S0-BJJ-044

3 1205 00566 0246

WITHDRAWN

TEENSTAGES

Parents' feedback

"I was feeling swamped with everything, really staggering from one day to the next. Grant and I both felt overloaded. But the six stages immediately made sense to us. Suddenly, all sorts of things came together that hadn't before. We were able to see how our teenagers needed different things from us, whereas before we'd been trying to do the same with them all. They [the stages] gave us a map to help us find our way through everything that was going on."

Angelica, mother of three teenagers

"I look back now and thank my lucky stars that I found out about the six stages. Knowing what was coming next meant that I was a little ahead of the game. And I was able to adjust and give my kid what she needed much more easily. I'm sure I would have missed far too much if I hadn't known about them."

Bernadette, single mother of Marie

"All the practical advice on what to do at the different stages was incredibly valuable. I felt I knew what to do. When your suggestions didn't work, by thinking a little I was usually able to come up with something that did."

Eckhard, father of two

These comments are typical of the benefits many have gained from using the information in the next six chapters, or their own adaptations of it. We hope that it will offer similar benefits to you.

TEENSTAGES

THE BREAKTHROUGH YEAR-BY-YEAR APPROACH TO UNDERSTANDING YOUR EVER-CHANGING TEEN

ELIZABETH & KEN MELLOR

SOURCEBOOKS, INC.®
NAPERVILLE, ILLINOIS

Copyright © 2004, 2009 by Biame Network, Inc.
Cover and internal design © 2009 by Sourcebooks, Inc.
Cover design by Cyanotype Book Architects
Cover photo © iStockPhoto.com/aldomurillo
Internal photos © Alex Coppel
Sourcebooks and the colophon are registered trademarks of Sourcebooks, Inc.

All rights reserved. No part of this book may be reproduced in any form or by any electronic or mechanical means including information storage and retrieval systems—except in the case of brief quotations embodied in critical articles or reviews—without permission in writing from its publisher, Sourcebooks, Inc.

This publication is designed to provide accurate and authoritative information in regard to the subject matter covered. It is sold with the understanding that the publisher is not engaged in rendering legal, accounting, or other professional service. If legal advice or other expert assistance is required, the services of a competent professional person should be sought.—*From a Declaration of Principles Jointly Adopted by a Committee of the American Bar Association and a Committee of Publishers and Associations*

All brand names and product names used in this book are trademarks, registered trademarks, or trade names of their respective holders. Sourcebooks, Inc., is not associated with any product or vendor in this book.

Published by Sourcebooks, Inc.
P.O. Box 4410, Naperville, Illinois 60567-4410
(630) 961-3900
Fax: (630) 961-2168
www.sourcebooks.com

Originally published in Australia in 2004 by Finch Publishing.

Library of Congress Cataloging-in-Publication Data

Mellor, Ken.
  Teen stages : the breakthrough year-by-year approach to understanding your ever-changing teen / Elizabeth & Ken Mellor.
       p. cm.
  Includes bibliographical references and index.
  1. Teenagers. 2. Adolescent psychology. 3. Parent and teenager. 4. Communication in the family. I. Mellor, Elizabeth J. (Elizabeth Jean), 1938- II. Title.
  HQ796.M398 2009
  155.5—dc22

                    2008048171

Printed and bound in the United States of America.
          UGI 10 9 8 7 6 5 4 3 2 1

Contents

155.5
MEL
cop.1

PUBLIC LIBRARY
DANVILLE, ILLINOIS

Introduction

So the time you have been waiting for is finally here! Your children are teenagers, at last! Have you been waiting with excitement or trepidation? Whatever you anticipated, you may be sure that they have almost certainly had their own fantasies. They are likely to have been hanging out for the "magical thirteen," when they could be called teenagers, with all the power, romance, and new beginnings that the word implies to the young. And it *is* magical, wonderful, and exciting. For many parents and teenagers, however, the teenage years are also challenging, hard, or very, very tough.

For most parents of teenagers and for teenagers themselves, the teenage years are a mix of both the splendid and the difficult.

Our purpose

Our primary reason for writing this book is to make the job of raising teenagers as easy and rewarding as we can. After more than 30 years of working, living, and playing with teenagers in a variety of settings, we have managed to collect an array of hints, answers to questions, ways of understanding what is happening, and specific techniques for dealing with particular issues and problems. We have also developed several overall approaches to guide the way we act as parents so the outcomes are as much what we want as we can make them.

The content

Many parents, teachers, youth workers, and professional helpers of one sort or another have tested our suggestions and found them helpful. We are not talking about formal research, however, but many hundreds of people following our suggestions while standing at the kitchen sink, driving the car, teaching in the classroom, in the middle of something beautiful, or in the midst of something horrible.

PUBLIC LIBRARY
DANVILLE, ILLINOIS

Significantly, many parents have raised their teenagers using this material to guide them. They have been delighted at how much easier the process became and what wonderful adults their children turned into. We have included lots of their comments, as well as the comments of other parents.

Main themes

We develop several themes throughout the book. You will find them clearly stated in many places, as well as embedded in the examples and suggestions that we make. They are:

★ *Loving connections need to be the foundations* on which everything else is built between parents and teenagers. This includes tough love.

★ *Parents are important.* There is no substitute for us and teenagers get into trouble without us. So we parents may need to reorganize ourselves to be available as much as is necessary.

★ *Great pleasure and joy arise* naturally throughout the teenage years. Celebrating these times is variously a relief, a way to strengthen resources for what comes next, and a reward for effort.

★ *Teenagers have a variety of needs* that can seem complicated and hard to meet. However, these needs are fairly easy to understand and to satisfy, making teenagers happier and easier to live with.

★ *Persistence and taking the long view are important.* We need to project ahead to see as much as we can the consequences of what we, and our teenage children, are doing or not doing.

★ *Parents are wise to work in teams* with co-parents, with parents of other teenagers, or with teachers. We are likely to have a much easier time than those trying to do everything alone.

★ *It is a tough journey for many.* That we, or our teenagers, are having trouble is not in itself a sign that we have anything wrong with us—or that they do. Facing challenges is normal for us all.

★ *The demands get easier as teenagers get older.* In many ways the demands of the teenage years are like those of the years from babyhood to late childhood. The rewards are similar too.

Developmental emphasis

A unique contribution of this book is our emphasis on teenage developmental stages. We have devoted about 60 percent of the book to them. Teenagers grow through a predictable sequence of stages during which their needs change very distinctively. Simply having information about these stages has been a wonderful confidence boost to many parents and other adults who had not previously realized how to explain the many shifts and changes that their teenagers were going through. With the information, they understood. Their relief was great, and they could look forward to what was likely to arise and back to what they had been through.

At the same time, the material on the stages highlights how important it is for parents and other adults to change what they do in parallel with the changes young people are going through. Our changes need to be specific to each stage so that we meet the needs arising in the young at each stage. And knowledge is power! When we adapt what we do to meet their needs, young people usually thrive. When we do not adapt, they usually get into difficulties.

Background

This book had its beginnings in 1996 when Rex and Vicki Finch approached us to write a book on teenagers. We were delighted and quickly set about the task. Thinking that it would need a good introduction that contained many of our general approaches to parenting, we started with it. Unexpectedly, the introduction rapidly developed a life of its own and turned into another book that was first published in 1999.

Now in its second edition, *ParentCraft: A practical guide to raising children well*, has many important suggestions and practical guidelines that are very helpful in raising teenagers. We have only included a few here and highly recommend that you have a look at *ParentCraft*. It covers all sorts of issues from conception to adulthood and we refer to it frequently in what follows.

Why "teenagers" and not "adolescents"?

The reason we chose to use the word "teenager" and not "adolescent" is simple. "Teenager" is the more commonly used word. At the same time, our selection does raise some issues that we need to address for the sake of clarity.

First, young people are considered teenagers from the time they turn thirteen until they turn twenty. By contrast, adolescence is usually considered to start with the hormonal surge that signals the beginning of puberty and to end at about twenty-one. In the past, these two systems were fairly well aligned. However, these days, they are not, because some children now enter puberty very much earlier. We discuss these issues in more detail in Section I.

Second, even had we decided to use the word "adolescent," we would still have related the six developmental stages to the age markers that we have used in Section III. In our experience, the age and stage matching that we present still holds true for enough young people to make using them well worthwhile. Having said this, it is still important to make the point that the ages given for each stage are only averages or guidelines. Many young people vary somewhat from them, some going into the stages earlier and some later. So we need to take care to consider teenagers as they are, not according to the material as presented.

Your part

We are satisfied that the information in this book is accurate and useful. That we are satisfied, however, does not guarantee that you will be, or that our suggestions will work for you or your teenager. So we urge you to test what you find here to ensure that it does apply to your family. Only you can do this. Fortunately, you can take things slowly. If you think something might help, make a small beginning, rather than going all out. Then, if you find things are improving, do more of what has worked. If not, try something else. Whatever you do, we wish you well.

Teenagers
and you

As parents of teenagers, we can use all the help we

can get. This section highlights several important

areas that need our attention and gives suggestions

on what to do about them. The areas include parental

responses to the advent of the teenage years, some

of the deeper forces stirring below the surface in our

young people's lives, some explanations as to why

the early teenage years are so very demanding, and

how important the community at large is to

teenagers.

CHAPTER 1

Teenager on board

The teenage years are a delight to many parents and other adults. They can see the unfolding miracle of life in the intense aliveness, sprouting bodies, good humor, expanding maturity, and evolving independence in their young people. They like teenagers and celebrate their talents and creativity. These adults take in their stride the ups and downs of dealing with the bursting energy, the vitality, and the challenges. Also, many parents look forward to sharing all sorts of wonderful experiences during this time, both with their co-parents and with their children.

This is not, however, the side of things that we tend to hear and see reported. Generally, we are exposed much more to parents and others who are struggling with or troubled by their teenagers. And given what teenagers often do, this is completely understandable.

The truth is that lots of parents have difficulty coping with the great variety of emotional, practical, and other pressures that arise naturally with teenagers. Many go through years of tension, worry, anguish, anger, fear, frustration, or hopelessness. These feelings arise as they try to manage and care for their teenagers, to keep them safe, and to help them learn to live in the grown-up world.

Parents could wear "Teenager on Board" signs, partly in pride, partly in warning, partly as a call for help!

An unexpected response

Here is a surprise. Many parents, even those at their wits' end, do not seek help. Given the level of discomfort caused and how long they endure it, this is remarkable. Naturally, as parent educators, we have wondered about the explanation for this, since help is at hand and so many people could avoid so much discomfort so easily.

Getting help is cool

Many, perhaps most, teenagers put lots of energy into keeping up appearances. It is very uncool for them to show that they are affected by what is going on around them. This might mean hiding their delight, ignorance, upset, confusion, doubt, interest in others, or their problems. At times, some go to enormous lengths to cover up their feelings.

Other common teenage responses to upset

★   *"I know I shouldn't feel this way."*

★   *"Sorry. I don't mean to cry."*

★   *"Leave me alone!"*

★   *"I can't help it . . . I'm sooo stupid."*

★   *"Don't take any notice."*

★   *"I'll be all right in a moment."*

★   *"I knew that."*

★   *Lapsing into silence, or walking away.*

Clearly, they need to get help at these times. This is probably more obvious to us than to them, however, because they are right in the middle of their own feelings and struggles. We could even spell it out for them, if they would listen: "I think you need to express those feelings. You aren't stupid. You're a wonderful person. Also, you need to learn how to take care of what causes the feelings. This only takes simple steps and we can take them together."

Put another way, we are saying, "Your problems can be solved; you're wonderful; you can do it; and I'll help." But it is so uncool for them to show any of this, or even to be upset in the first place, that as parents we may need to act with considerable determination to get through their "barriers." Happily, as we persist sensitively, teenagers generally respond by opening up, learning what they need to, and becoming more relaxed about showing what is going on with them. This can take years!

The uncool virus

While this kind of resistance is familiar to parents and to adults who have a lot to do with teenagers, there is something that many adults do not know. We can easily catch the uncool virus ourselves from teenagers or other parents. It is highly contagious. Transmission occurs simply through talking and other social contact. And the consequences are potentially serious, both for us and for the teenagers.

Parental symptoms of the uncool virus

★ *pretending to friends that we're coping when we aren't*

★ *acting as if we know things we don't know*

★ *suppressing upset feelings, particularly in public*

★ *arguing with others who do things differently*

★ *feeling increasing desperation, depression, or anxiety*

★ *withdrawing while at home*

★ *staying away out of reluctance to go home*

★ *acting out angrily inside the family.*

Above all, the main symptom is that we do not seek the help we need. In other words, we act like teenagers. So what is the cure?

Seeking help

Somehow, in the midst of our reluctance, embarrassment, uncertainties, self-consciousness, frustrations, fears, doubts, or hopes that things will change for the better very soon, we need to get ourselves to act. We need to be willing to act uncool, so we can solve our problems. Once we have, we will generally realize that seeking help was not as risky as it seemed it would be before we acted.

Acting uncool means acting sensibly.

Fortunately, there are lots of options for finding help, including:

★ books, magazines, newspapers

★ experienced relatives or friends

★ parenting classes and courses

★ movies

★ chatrooms and bulletin and notice boards (on the Internet)

★ whole websites on parenting teenagers

★ professional advice

★ parent advice groups and telephone services.

However, to decide to get help, we need to understand that it is worthwhile. Simply knowing what is available is not always enough. Only direct experience truly works. So, if you need help, we urge you to go and get it, even if it is not easy for you.

Good reasons to get help instead of waiting

★ *Many problems, even serious ones, have simple solutions.*

★ *The sooner we act, the easier it will be to change things.*

★ *No matter how cool others look to us, just about all parents of teenagers understand how hard it is at times.*

★ *We don't have to keep struggling—help is at hand.*

★ *We have lots of company; we are not alone.*

★ *What is unresolved now will continue into the future, until it is worked out, usually getting more serious the longer it goes on.*

★ *Teenagers want the relief we crave as much as we do, even if they won't show it, or say so.*

★ *Many parents feel pushed, sometimes very, very pushed.*

★ *Getting advice on parenting is not therapy, so there doesn't have to be anything "wrong" with us for us to seek help.*

★ *The relief we can feel when we learn to manage things differently is incredibly wonderful and makes whatever we need to do to get it worthwhile.*

★ *Life with teenagers is much easier, often fantastic, when we are managing ourselves well with them.*

★ *We can all learn to manage better.*

CHAPTER 2

What comes next?

The advent of the teenage years signals the last stage of childhood. Twelve years have already passed, almost thirteen if we include the pregnancy. Only eight years remain until our children reach full emotional maturity. We are in the home stretch!

Heaving a sigh of relief, lots of parents these days pull back. They believe that they have reached the point where they can reduce their parental responsibilities very significantly. However, the end of our responsibilities needs to come much more gradually.

An understandable reaction

Parental reactions and beliefs like these are easily understood. Young people at twelve seem fairly mature, self-contained, and organized. They often have very clear ideas about who they are and what they think is important in life. They are often available to, and capable of taking care of younger children and doing a good job, as long as they only have to do it for limited periods. They are also often socially responsible and interested in influencing the world around them. Of course, not all are like this. Many are challenging, argumentative, somewhat prejudiced, and very inclined to boss others around. Some are a mixture of maturity and these other qualities.

In the face of their maturity, parents frequently conclude that the coming years will simply involve an extension of what has gone before. All that we anticipate we will need to do is to tie up a few loose ends. We are certainly not thinking that our teenage children will require even more input from us than they have for some years.

Twelve-year-olds can seem so mature to many parents that they pull back and spend less time with their children. Unfortunately, this is the opposite of what young teenagers need.

A chance for more work or play

Prompted by these ideas, increasing numbers of parents start reorganizing their lives to take on more work. Others, who have not worked for years, find jobs. And many parents without work expand their existing activities, enjoying the chance to do more of what they find personally satisfying away from home. "Now they are almost grown up, we can stay away and work or enjoy ourselves more."

Naturally, increasing family income seems sensible. The extra money would provide welcome assistance in meeting the high costs of raising families and would enable everyone to enjoy attractive opportunities that would otherwise remain unavailable. And the extra stimulation available outside our homes could draw us powerfully in that direction as well.

Acting with the best of intentions

Our impression is that most parents who pull back do so with the best of intentions. We may think, for example, that it will encourage and respect their independence. And keeping track of them while we think like this may seem like "interference," so we restrain ourselves.

Also well intentioned, other parents pull back for a different range of reasons. They try to stay involved, but are met with silence, active withdrawal, tantrums, sullenness, hassling, violence or threats of violence, or other forms of manipulation. Greeted by responses that are clearly intended to get us to stop "interfering" and to leave our teenagers alone, many of us do just that. Lots of parents feel challenged, intimidated, or overwhelmed by responses like these. Others of us are fearful that our teenagers will, for example, run away from home or put themselves at risk in other ways, if we persist. So we pull back under these circumstances to avoid the exchanges that might precipitate problems.

In practice, pulling back rarely works to avoid problems, and usually leads to others.

Ways we leave teenagers alone too much

When everyone is regularly under the same roof, we may think we are having lots to do with our children. However, the reverse may be true without our noticing it. Here are some ways we may leave them alone inappropriately:

★ *not talking much to them and leaving them to themselves in their rooms for long periods*

★ *not checking generally what they are doing day by day*

★ *not getting detailed information on outings before they leave*

★ *not finding out where they are after school, or who is visiting them at home*

★ *not taking the time to celebrate their enjoyments, interests, and successes*

★ *not pressing on with discussions of upsets when they show reluctance*

★ *not making sure they are going to school every day*

★ *not keeping track of how well they are doing at school*

★ *not monitoring the TV programs, videos, movies, and DVDs they watch*

★ *not censoring the books and magazines they read, or the computer and other games they play*

★ *not spending time with them immediately before they leave for, or as they arrive home from, school*

★ *not having family time with them*

★ *not investigating what they do on the Internet: the websites they visit, the chatrooms they frequent, or the regular email systems they enroll in.*

What teenagers actually need

Teenagers actually need us to move in closer, not to pull back—to spend more time with them, not less. The reason is that they go through many major changes at about the age of thirteen. From then on, they are forever different, a fact that neither we nor they can change. And they depend on us to accept their emerging needs and passions, and to help them to learn to manage themselves anew.

CHAPTER 3

The switch

John was talking at a workshop we ran on teenagers:

"My daughter was the first to go through the switch in our family and I took a while to realize what was happening. Now, looking back, I realize that her transformation was really quick. One day she was the way she'd been for years and the next she was different. I didn't seem to know her anymore, although this was more a suspicion in the background in the beginning than something I really understood. I started to feel uncertain of myself with her and I'd never felt that way— ever. Also, she would flare up at whoever was there for no apparent reason. For a while I just kept doing what I had always done. I guess I hoped the changes would pass. But they didn't. I felt dislocated from her, and I felt the loss of the ease I used to have with her."

"It was the sudden neediness that really got to me," Mary said passionately at the same workshop. "I was looking forward to getting on with my life, then Garry went through the switch. Whereas before this I hardly saw him, suddenly I couldn't get rid of him. I'd sit on the couch and he'd be right there jammed up against me. And he kept asking me to tell him what to do—things he'd known for years. I was really irritated. But I also felt guilty for feeling this; something told me he really needed my attention. I didn't handle it very well, either. I really resented the extra time he demanded."

In our experience, all teenagers go through some kind of marked transformation. Usually beginning at about thirteen years of age, once begun, "the switch," as we call it, tends to grow stronger and more obvious as the years pass.

How quickly the switch occurs varies. Some teenagers make it overnight, others make it more gradually. The changes themselves also vary greatly (see Section III). In this chapter, we explore common parental reactions to and general explanations of the switch.

Common parental reactions

How we react as parents to our children during and after the switch is as variable as the reactions of teenagers themselves. Also, while not all of us react strongly, strong reactions are common. Whatever the level of our responses, they arise as we do our best to adjust to the new "rules," reactions, expectations, and emotional demands our growing children introduce into our lives.

> ### *Common parental responses to the switch*
>
> ★ *trying to understand and doing what makes sense*
>
> ★ *not noticing and pressing on with life as before*
>
> ★ *feeling disconcerted, upset, or at a loss to know what to do*
>
> ★ *doing nothing different and hoping everything will work out*
>
> ★ *worrying that something is wrong with our teenagers or us*
>
> ★ *getting argumentative, angry, or punitive with them*
>
> ★ *disciplining them as if they can or should change back*
>
> ★ *feeling as if it is all too hard*
>
> ★ *denying anything is different*
>
> ★ *getting busy with other activities*
>
> ★ *trying to soothe and appease them*
>
> ★ *feeling relief at the second chance that has arrived.*

Partly, of course, the challenge of the switch is that we are not consulted before it occurs. Suddenly we find ourselves along for a different ride from the one we thought we were on. In addition, we are having to play catch-up and many of us feel wrong-footed by this. Instead of the measure of control we used to have when our children were younger, we now feel as if much of our lives are lived at their whim. Adding to the challenge, we may also feel as if we have to deal with someone who is bigger than we are, and not as subject to our influence anymore.

Common explanations

Several key factors are usually presented to explain why teenagers change. These can help parents to understand what is going on. They are:

★ surging hormones

★ growth spurts

★ intense and changeable feelings

★ expanding life experience

★ desire for independence.

Hormones   Puberty begins with the release of hormones into young bodies that have never experienced their effects before. For girls it is estrogen and for boys testosterone. While young people do not usually understand their influence directly, in the beginning at least, powerful forces start to emerge within them. With this explanation, the hormones are seen as responsible for, or associated with, the other physical and emotional changes that occur at the same time.

Growth spurts   Both boys and girls go through accelerated growth at around thirteen. Some, particularly the girls, tend to do this earlier. All the same, most will grow rapidly somewhere between the ages of ten and fifteen. They may become much taller very quickly, body hair starts to appear, breasts bud and develop, penises mature, and boys find their voices breaking. All face adjusting to how different they look to themselves and others and to the initial awkwardness, or gawkiness, of physically managing bigger, longer boned bodies. Then, too, they need to handle all the comparisons, often anxious or negative, that they make between themselves and others.

Feelings   The early teenage years are punctuated by intense and changing feelings. On some days, our young can act with happiness, poise, and balance, only to act erratically and to feel great distress, anger, or fear the next. For young teenagers these rapid changes are perfectly normal. Even so, the teenagers themselves are often at a loss to explain what is going on. They can feel just as disconcerted and upset, or more so, by their reactions as we do. Girls have the added dimension of having to learn to experience and deal with the emotional changes that accompany their menstrual cycles, once they begin.

Life experience   Much more is expected of young people in their early teenage years than previously. They go to high schools, which are often bigger, more impersonal, and more demanding than they are accustomed to. They are the youngest again, too, instead of the oldest as they were at the end of elementary school. At the same time, as mentioned, parents are often expecting more self-reliance than previously. The learning involved in all of this requires effort and may produce stress.

Independence   Underlying much of what they experience is the desire to strike out on their own. They can now see other young people who are older doing things that seem wonderfully attractive. They are beginning to feel a sense of power in themselves that is new and intriguing. The bigger pond of high school and their developing maturity open new, previously unknown options. Somehow they need to learn to manage all this.

Also, they often start to compare us with other parents and adults. Their wider experience naturally leads to this. With comparison comes criticism and the need then to adjust to their new views of their parents. Considering that they need us more, this development is not well timed, comfortable, or welcome. However, it is what we may have to deal with along with the other changes.

Dealing with the challenge

In our experience, the best response overall is to learn to juggle competing demands, not easy to do at times. For example:

★ Move in and engage quickly; avoid hanging back lest you intrude.

★ Notice what they do and set clear standards and limits.

★ Challenge them when they go "over the top," and remain open.

★ Expect them to act sensitively with others and teach them to take a stand on important matters. Persist in making contact with them even if they resist, and understand that resistance is an "invitation to persist."

CHAPTER 4
Becoming young again

The explanations in the last chapter do help us to understand our teenagers. They are important aspects of what is going on for them and so for us. However, much mystery remains until we consider several other key factors. We will do so in this and the following two chapters. This extra information can help us to understand much more of what our teenagers are going through. And, very importantly, our greater understanding can help us to clarify what our teenagers actually need and how to supply it effectively.

Regressiveness

Teenagers have an unfolding series of lessons to learn about themselves, other people, and the world they will eventually live in as adults. The demands of these lessons gradually expand as young people get older and more is expected of them.

> ### *Examples of important teenage lessons*
>
> ★ *to learn to develop bodily mastery and grace*
>
> ★ *to manage increasingly complex intellectual tasks at school*
>
> ★ *to relate to peers as sexual people*
>
> ★ *to begin to figure out who they are as people*
>
> ★ *to have ideas about their place in the world and what they will do with their lives.*

At the same time, and as part of doing all of this, they also need to grow up all over again. This need arises because at around the age of thirteen they regress emotionally. They then revert to thinking, feeling, and acting much younger than they now are.

People often explain these changes in terms of the effects of the hormonal surge; however, it is more than that. Their regression involves a deep shift that takes them emotionally back to babyhood again, at least in parts of them. This may seem like a strange claim, particularly when we think of how big their bodies are and how they can talk and think and do other things that fairly grown-up children can do. Nevertheless, thirteen-year-olds often begin to resemble babies in many ways.

What is very surprising to many parents is that their children were previously so competent in all areas.

"My thirteen-year-old wasn't like that," many parents have claimed. And they are right about what they noticed. The regression is less marked in some teenagers than in others. There are some who remain very poised, balanced, and mature. However, we need to understand that, immediately after the switch, no matter how externally mature teenagers seem, they partly experience their lives as babies do.

Common changes associated with regressiveness

★ acting more affectionately and lovingly

★ feeling more needy than before

★ getting deeply and disproportionately distressed or angry

★ possibly crying a lot more than usual

★ feeling unable to cope

★ needing to rely on others to help them feel better

★ finding their attention span has contracted

★ discovering previously simple tasks are more difficult

★ having difficulty remembering and losing track of time.

We repeat: some young people are touched like this only slightly. Even so, in our experience, all are touched to some extent. Once used to the idea, many of us feel relieved. We can understand more clearly why young teenagers are so capable one moment and so dependent the next. They are both capable *and* dependent.

Two levels of growth

Our teenagers have begun to live on two levels at the same time—as teenagers and as much younger children. It is important to accept their new dependency and respond to it. We can neither ignore these young needs without doing damage to the young people ignored, nor can we hurry the regrowth process, which takes its own time. (See Section III for details of the sequence of stages they grow through.)

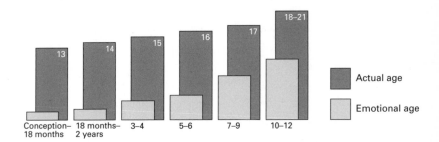

All of these factors mean that teenagers need to do two things. First, they need to regrow emotionally through all the younger stages of their lives. The above diagram shows the young "regressed ages" and how they generally match their actual ages. Second, and at the same time, they need to negotiate the teenage-related learning that faces them as they continue to get older. It is a big task.

What teenagers need from parents

Our job is to respond to both levels of need. To deal with their regressiveness, we have to provide the intensity of contact, nurturing, and other parenting that they need in order for the younger parts of them to grow up again. If we do, they grow. Very importantly, if we do not respond with what they need, then they can get very stuck. They may stay emotionally as children instead of maturing to adulthood.

To deal with the age-related learning, we have to be there for them so they can engage us with feeling, and intellectually, socially, and spiritually. It is a big world out there and we, as their parents, are their primary informants, teachers, and consultants about what is there and how to deal with it. We are also the people most connected to them genetically or emotionally, and so are usually best placed to help them to find themselves and to develop firm inner foundations. Other adults play their parts, but they are not as primary, initially at least.

CHAPTER **5**
Brain changes

Naturally, you may wonder why teenagers regress as described in the last chapter. We certainly did for many years. That they did was obvious. That their regrowth followed the same sequence as children grow through in their first twelve years was also obvious. Similarly, it was obvious that teenagers whose needs were met at the two levels mentioned in the last chapter did very much better than those who missed out on having their needs met at either level.

An unexpected answer

Unexpectedly, we read a summary in the *New Scientist* of some very exciting research findings into children's brain development. The research found that at about ten to twelve years of age the brain showed a surge of growth (girls a little before boys). The brain areas involved had to do with "social judgment and self-control." Moreover, this surge meant that the brains of young teenagers closely resembled the brains of newborn babies in important ways. Of further interest was that the findings showed that subsequent changes in the brain were not completed until the early twenties.

It is no wonder, then, that some young teenagers begin to act, think, and feel like babies again. Their central nervous systems have rewired themselves to make this very likely. Also, it is no wonder that the consequent emotional, social, and other developmental needs continue until young people are in their early twenties. It takes that long for the new brain areas to be reprogrammed or rewired, and stabilized through experience.

Programming the brain

A wondrous organ, the human brain is beautifully designed so that we arrive on the planet with some generalized wiring or circuitry already in place. This is enough to keep us alive and to manage as babies, provided that our mothers and fathers, or others in their stead, care for us. More than this is required though, because to survive as we get older we need to refine and develop this wiring.

Our life experiences do this. The repetitive movements babies make, as well as the repetition of instructions, encouragement, limit setting, and the other things that we do with young children, are all involved. The repetition is important here. It is through this that the necessary nerve fibers are formed and consolidated. And it is these fibers that enable children to maintain what they are learning. Did you ever wonder why you had to repeat yourself so often for your children to learn even simple things?

Reprogramming the teenage brain

The same processes are required for the teenage brain to develop. We need to take teenagers repeatedly through the "drills" that program their new brain areas. Significantly, these are to do with self-control, social awareness and maturity, and self-management and planning. In other words, we need to resocialize our teenage children. And the way they act shows us this very clearly at times.

Does this take you back to when your children were babies, toddlers, and young children? It should, because their needs are very similar.

As with babies and young children, we have very important parts to play in teenage reprogramming. Without our involvement, teenage brains will not develop normally. This is very much related to the need for our involvement that we mentioned in the last chapter. The parallels between young children and teenagers are remarkable!

Generally, what they need is physical, emotional, cognitive, and spiritual learning—repeated as many times as necessary for the rewiring to occur. All the conversations and other exchanges about the insignificant and significant things in life are part of this.

The teenage "software" upgrade

We can explain some of what is going on clearly by noticing the parallels with computers. The analogy is not far-fetched. Think of teenagers as "human bio-computers." Now imagine that the life experience of their first twelve years installs "software" called "Living Life—Child Programs." This software contains all sorts of instructions on how to handle the various inner experiences, people, situations, and events that they encounter in their lives.

If you are familiar enough with computers, you will know that software becomes out of date due to various types of changes. Some are changes in hardware. These usually result from advances in technology, like developing faster gadgets for doing the calculations. Other changes are connected with what we start to want our computers to do some time after we get them, for example, when we expect them to do something different from what they currently can. The point is that old software often does not work in more advanced computers. Also, old software is frequently not designed to handle the new jobs we now want our computers to do. The only solution is to upgrade.

The same applies to "teenage human bio-computers." They need upgrades. During childhood, their systems become increasingly sophisticated. And, while successive modifications of the "Living Life" software are carried out to cope with these changes, they are not geared to the highly sophisticated "bio-computer" that appears in the early teenage years. Just think of the differences in capacity between a two-year-old child and a fourteen-year-old, for example. Also, think of how much more is expected of children as they get older.

The upgrade process starts at about thirteen years of age. The upgraded "software" is called "Living Life—Adult Programs" and it takes about seven years to install.

Many parents are convinced of the value of this information about regressiveness and brain changes. Here is a selection of what they have said.

Parents wise up to brain changes

"It was such a relief to find out why he was acting so strangely. I was really worried and thought that there must have been something wrong."

"Knowing that the changes go on for years was a bit daunting at first. But it made things a lot easier later on, because I realized what the kids were doing was normal and I was prepared for it to take a long time."

"I didn't know that I needed to start again with my first son and he has really struggled. But with my others I did know and the differences are fantastic. Thank goodness I found out in time for them."

"My son is fourteen and fully into the struggles you describe. But now I'm feeling much more confident in standing my ground with him because I know it's what he needs, just like when he was two."

"When I heard about the brain stuff, I had the thought, 'Hit the gym, or your muscles don't get strong,' and it all made sense to me. So when I get irritated at having to repeat things over and over, I remember that every time I do my kids' brains are becoming a little more developed."

"Phew. How can I deal with all of this? I now realize how much I might have to do with my teenage kids. We're probably going to have to reorganize ourselves very significantly to be there for them."

"Knowing the different stages and what to do was essential. Without that information, I would have been lost. It was a great road map that helped us get to the end."

CHAPTER **6**

The life cycle and its transitions

Take a few moments to think back over your life. Notice when your activities, interests, and energies have ebbed and when they have flowed. Do you remember times when you were very reflective, turned inward, slowed down, and liked to sit around a lot or do very little? You will probably also remember when you were filled with vitality, very taken up with your external life, keen to stay busy, and enjoyed getting involved in projects and outside interests. How long did these times last?

We all go through a repeating cycle that has profound effects on our lives. Teenagers (and younger children) are as subject to its impact as any of us. Understanding its influences, particularly in the early and late teenage years, is very important. Doing so enables us to help young people to deal with deeply unsettling issues that can surface at these times. Resolving these issues is fundamental to their inner stability and to their general well-being. In fact, for some, their very lives may depend on our responses.

The life cycle

Just as the tides in our oceans and the way we breathe ebb and flow, so our life energies ebb and flow. For most people, these are subtle, almost nonexistent changes, although many are able to recognize them immediately once they are alerted to them.

Our systems seem to breathe. For a time, they breathe in; then for a time, they breathe out. At this point, the whole cycle repeats itself. Each "half breath" takes seven years, with one complete "breath" taking fourteen years. Because it takes so long, we can easily understand why many people miss the cycle. The "substance" we breathe is "vital force," or "life energy." Whatever this is, it animates us and feeds our aliveness. It also prompts and guides our growth and development. It is the force behind the unfolding miracle of life that we can observe in our children.

To help you to recognize this more fully in your own life, let's return to the exercise you did at the beginning of the chapter.

People in their late twenties to mid-thirties and in their early to late forties are generally inwardly directed, that is, they are "breathing in." They usually prefer, even crave, the opportunity to slow down and live fairly laid-back, relaxed lives.

Young adults in their early to late twenties and older adults from their mid-thirties to early forties generally thrive on the "busyness" of life and seek out activity. They are "breathing out."

More about the cycle

During the inward phase, or "in breath," we are inwardly directed. Our natural preferences are to live in slowed down sorts of ways, resting, reflecting, and taking time for ourselves. We prefer others to take initiative and to come to us, rather than us taking it or going to them. Routine activities are much easier than those requiring active creativity and intervention. Drawing others towards us is much easier than our going toward them. Also, the sources of our creativity, ideas, and awareness of what is needed seem to arise "from the depths" of us, rather than from active, deliberate, analytical processing.

During the outward phase, or "out breath," we are outwardly directed. Our natural preferences are to live actively, to engage with the world around us, to do things that make a difference to others and the world, to initiate projects and to follow through until they are complete. We are much more inclined to stay physically active than to slow down. We are stimulated by challenges and enjoy involvement with others. Our creativity and other talents arise naturally as part of analysis, active intervention with others, and our external involvement with situations, events, and issues in the outside world.

The childhood cycle

Prior to entering their teens, children have already been through one full cycle. From conception to a few months after their sixth birthday, they are in an inwardly directed phase. Think of how much time and energy babies and young children require, how much the world revolves around what they need and feel, and how absorbed in themselves they are.

This seven-year period is followed by an active, outwardly directed phase that lasts for just as long. During this phase, children's attention and learning occur much more in the world. They get involved in school, with their friends and other children, and with learning how to do things. They need to learn to persist until they complete tasks and to find their place with their peers. This phase generally ends after they turn thirteen.

The teenage phase   How is this information about cycles relevant to teenagers? We want to make two points. First, the teenage years coincide with a complete seven-year, inwardly directed phase. It begins at about thirteen and ends at about twenty years of age.

We have found little indication that this is triggered by puberty. The overall cycle begins at conception and seems to flow through our lives with predictable regularity. Although at this stage it seems most unlikely to us that puberty influences the timing of the thirteen-year-old transition into the inward phase, it may. In other words, we are not sure enough to say that it has no effect, but so far we have seen little evidence to show that it does.

Many signs indicate this transition to the inward phase, and the following are common:

★ From being relatively low maintenance and outwardly directed as they approach twelve, our children become increasingly high maintenance after they turn thirteen.

★ They begin to draw lots of energy toward them from the outside.

★ They usually become very self-absorbed.

★ Many of them want to spend lots of time watching TV, being entertained by other low-demand activities, or sleeping.

★ They engage us intensely in ways that demand responses and, therefore, energy from us.

These tendencies are natural. Accepting their need to go inwards, therefore, is helpful, although we do need to ensure that teenagers are active in their lives too. A general approach that works well is to allow time for "going in" and, at the same time, ensure that they stay actively engaged in all areas of their lives that demand attention.

The second point relates to the periods of transition between the phases. These are very disturbing for many people. They occur when our systems move from "breathing out" to "breathing in," or from "breathing in" to "breathing out."

The times of transition are often accompanied by very disturbing challenges or problems.

Transitions

Between one phase and the next, we go through a transitional period. This is an "at rest" time. Our energies have little or no direction during these periods. It just seems to sit still.

Basics about transitions and the cycle

The transitions are the "times between," times of stillness, not of flow. Our energies are "at rest." As we go through these periods, we experience little natural inclination or motivation for anything very much. Also, these transitions themselves take time, mostly up to two years, although occasionally more.

During the phases themselves, our inclinations and motivations are markedly different. Within each phase, the intensity and flow of our energies usually incline us to do things. The intensity increases gradually until about half-way through each phase when it is at its maximum. After this, it gradually decreases to nothing again as we move into the next transition period.

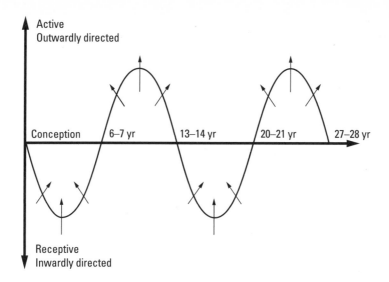

In the diagram you can see the way this works. Notice the clear transitions at six to seven, thirteen to fourteen, and twenty to twenty-one years of age. The first, at six to seven years of age, is from inwardly directed to outwardly directed living. The second, at thirteen to fourteen years of age, is from outwardly to inwardly directed living.

Notice, too, the transition at the end of the teenage years. The phase that follows is another active, outwardly directed one, and this is a natural time for young adults to go out into the world to get established.

Transition experiences
During a transition we often lose the sense of direction or flow that we were previously aware of. This loss can easily lead to a loss of confidence in ourselves. People do identify themselves with the flow of activity and "busyness," or with the flow of receptivity and reflectiveness. So for some people the loss of flow seems to dissolve their sense of identity and purpose and affects them greatly.

Some respond with equanimity and confidence, enjoying the time to experience themselves more deeply. However, many experience themselves as drifting, rootless, purposeless, and lost during this time. Some become disturbed to the very core.

To put it another way, when the tides of our energies no longer flow in or out, our deeper selves emerge in the resulting stillness. Like seaweed floating up as the tide turns, our subterranean needs and desires surface. Many old feelings, thoughts, attitudes, memories, beliefs, and decisions about ourselves float up into our awareness.

Value in the transition times

Transition times are wonderful opportunities to embrace what we like about ourselves. They also enable us to face and to come to terms with the less pleasant aspects we discover about ourselves. We can certainly learn from both.

If what floats to the surface is filled with happiness, contentment, love, fulfilment, self-confidence, or a sense of self-worth, then we are likely to welcome these times. Less welcome and comfortable are feelings, memories, and experiences of trauma, uncertainty, pain, disturbance, unhappiness, or difficulty.

Trauma in transition   Uncomfortable experiences are, in fact, fairly common. Some are fairly mild, others are very unsettling. Those going through deeply troubling experiences may face periods of extreme challenge, soul-searching, self-doubt, "lostness," and questioning the value of keeping on living. Of great importance here is that many teenagers are affected in this way. Just because they are young, they are not immune. So we need to remain alert at both the beginning and the end of the teenage years for signs of difficulty from this source.

The so-called "mid-life crisis" is a well-known adult transition time.

The troubled thirteen-year-old

Sam went through a time of flaring up with a kind of heated desperation. Particularly when he was in trouble with his parents, or having difficulty with kids at school, he would lash out at someone and end by saying, "I'm useless; I don't want to be alive anymore."

Upset thirteen-year-olds often become preoccupied with themselves and their deeply felt emotions. At the most extreme, their whole lives can begin to revolve around a kind of torture that they put themselves through. Examples along these lines include:

★ "I can't cope."

★ "I'm hopeless (a waste of space, evil)."

★ "No one should love me (like me, value me)."

★ "Is there something wrong with me?"

★ "I may as well die."

★ "I'm not worth it and everyone will find out—then what?"

★ "I wish I'd never been born."

For some, these traumas are fairly mild and occur only occasionally. For others, while more intense, they are more spasmodic, only arising when they get very upset about something. However, some troubled unfortunates are rarely happy. A small number are so miserable that they can become actively suicidal if not helped. Remember, too, that these kinds of experiences can go on for as long as two years.

The troubled twenty-year-old

Kris became very dejected about the world and all the defects he could see in it. He worried incessantly and, while seeking real answers, he felt sure nothing would work. In the midst of this time he decided, "This is no world to bring children into." And he kept this decision for the rest of his life.

Upset twenty-year–olds are more preoccupied with the state of the world and whether or not it is worthwhile. They may feel upset about themselves too; however, this is generally not primary. They can become deeply troubled, even obsessed, with how to change things for the better in the world. Self-worth and soul-searching are very much a part of this as they try to work out how to make the best contribution that they possibly can. Flavored with great personal uncertainty, the kinds of issues that arise include:

★ "What does it all mean?"

★ "The world's hopeless (going to hell, wrecked)."

★ "Life's not worth it (is full of suffering)."

PUBLIC LIBRARY
DANVILLE, ILLINOIS

★ "Everything I think of doing is meaningless."

★ "It's all too big for me."

★ "I want to contribute, but how can I?"

As with thirteen-year-olds, the range of responses varies greatly. Some young adults ask these questions and, even given their uncertainties, answer them fairly easily and quickly. Others have periods of anguished or angry soul-searching that, nevertheless, pass fairly quickly. Then there are those who get caught in the process and need lots of help to move through it. As with thirteen-year-olds, they may become seriously disturbed and need outside help.

What they need from parents

As mentioned, while very upsetting for some, the process of going through these transitions is very healing. Many wonderful outcomes are possible, provided the transition periods are managed well. Primarily, teenagers are revisiting feelings and decisions from long ago that are still influencing them. The solution is to learn to accept their feelings about themselves and revise their old opinions—producing profound change.

Basically teenagers need and value our availability and commitment to helping them through the processes they are experiencing. Our presence with them is important for this. And even if it goes on for years, our persistence helps to promote theirs. There are several key responses that we recommend:

★ Accept what they say they are experiencing.

★ Affirm: "You are upset."

★ Avoid as a first step trying to persuade them that they are wrong, even if they are. Wait and give them time to talk.

★ Hear them out and encourage them to express themselves—even their intense feelings.

★ Only begin rational discussion after they have expressed their feelings. Doing otherwise often gives them the impression that we don't understand, or aren't really interested in them.

★ Give clear feedback, stay open, practical, and matter-of-fact.

Specific things parents can do to help

For troubled thirteen-year-olds:

★ *Repeat basic messages like "I love you," "You're a worthwhile person," "You'll learn to cope with things," "I'm here and will help you," "You'll start to feel better about yourself soon," "Your feelings are not who you are."*

★ *Give clear direction to them about how to deal with the feelings and other experiences they are having and the conclusions they have drawn.*

★ *Spend time with them. They need to know that we are there for them—they get this from our physical presence.*

For troubled twenty-year-olds:

★ *Repeat basic messages like "This time will pass," "I love you and value you as a person," "I think you'll work out what's important," "I know you have a contribution to make," "Take your time; I'm confident you'll work out what you need to do in your life," "There's lots about the world that's worthwhile."*

★ *Discuss the issues with them receptively, and express opinions directly without trying to impose them.*

Spend time hanging out with them when they are going through these periods. We may need to look for opportunities. Avoid trying to come up with the answers for them. All the same, continue to express your views with "I-statements," such as those above.

CHAPTER **7**

Why all the strife?

"Our youth now love luxury, they have bad manners, contempt for authority; they show disrespect for their elders and love chatter in places of exercise. They no longer rise when others enter the room. They contradict their parents, chatter before company, gobble their food, and tyrannize their teachers."

SOCRATES—5TH CENTURY BCE

The early teenage years are "famous" for struggle and strife. We see it portrayed in movies, on TV, in books, and in magazines. Their distress, surly looks, red faces, strident voices, pouting mouths, "try and make me" words, and disappearing backs with neck and shoulders set in defiant concrete are all so common at this stage. Parents, teachers, and other carers, in particular, face this kind of thing regularly. And as the Socrates' quote shows, these themes have been around for millennia.

The impression we can easily get as parents from the media portrayals is of a certain inevitability about this kind of behavior and almost no understanding of what is behind it. At the same time, what parents do is usually shown as not making much difference. Their actions seem ineffectual and they seem out of their depth.

In this chapter we explain why we think teenagers act as they do at fourteen years of age and make preliminary suggestions for dealing with what they do. We think that what is going on is easily understood and what they need becomes obvious once we do understand. For the sake of balance, of course, it is important to mention again that some young people are wonderful at this age. They, however, are generally not the ones who challenge us.

Fourteen-year-olds are going through a very demanding stage. If they get what they need, they will move on. If not, they will most probably get stuck.

Revisiting regressiveness

As we mentioned in Chapter 4, teenagers regress emotionally to some extent at thirteen years of age and go through a process of growing up again during the following seven years. As we explained, with some teenagers this is very obvious and "on the surface," while with others it is more an undercurrent in what they are doing.

For both groups, the regressive aspect and their need to grow up again are significant. First, during the teenage years they revisit each developmental stage that they went through from conception to late childhood. Second, at the same time, they are also growing through their "purely teenage" experiences. They need to do both to reach adulthood fully formed. We describe the way this richness unfolds in some detail in Section III.

Before we get to the more detailed descriptions there, however, we want to prepare the way with special emphasis on what is happening with fourteen-year-olds. This understanding leads naturally to a special understanding of fifteen-year-olds as well, which we will describe in the next chapter. First, however, we need to go back in time to when your children were little. Remember that much of what we deal with during the teenage years comes from back then.

The early years with children

The most demanding, labor-intensive time with our young is generally when they are babies, toddlers, and young children. The demands change gradually and reduce through that time. However, they usually remain high until children are about six and have been at school for a couple of years.

Babies   Young babies are totally dependent on us for everything that comes from the outside. They are unable to survive alone and need our care and attention. As they grow, they gradually become more mobile, physically capable, aware of other people, verbal, and they begin to understand feelings.

Toddlers   By the end of eighteen months, during which we have given them a great deal of time and attention, toddlers understandably have the distinct impression that everything in the world revolves around them. Their needs, desires, and preferences have very much set our agendas up to this age. This is appropriate and lays an ideal foundation for good self-esteem.

Young children   This "idyllic" state of affairs is about to change, however. At about eighteen months, toddlers enter a new phase during which they move from babyhood to young childhood. They often start to "hold out" and struggle with us, where previously they were amenable and cooperative. At times, much of what they do involves tantrums, resistance, and passion. During some days they manage to flavor almost everything with anger. Also, they often "work at" feeling disgruntled and upset and, at those times, are usually unavailable to our attempts to distract or console them.

> ### *The birth at two years of age*
>
> *"The terrible twos," a common title for this time, captures quite well the flavor of the struggling aspect of what they do. However, there is much more to it than this. We think that describing the process as a birth does much more justice to what is going on. The parallels between the sequence two-year-olds go through and physical birth are remarkable. The difference is that at two the birth is an emotional one, not a physical one.*

The emotional birth of the child   Taking the main aspects of physical birth, the way this second birth works is very easy to understand. Here is how it goes.

The start   The birth begins at the point children become resistant and determined to persist in making life "difficult" for themselves and others. They get upset and seem to "want" to feel that way.

The contractions   Their resistance is "wonderfully crafted" to get us (mothers and fathers) to resist too. Their emotion-packed behavior stimulates parents to feel impatient and to want to demand more of them than we have previously. And this is what we do. We begin to expect more of them, and we start actively to shape their behavior so that they meet our expectations. Our mutual struggles are the contractions:

★ "Wait a minute. I'm busy right now."

★ "Talk to me in a normal voice; don't snivel at me."

★ "You'll have to walk beside me, I can't carry you at the moment; my hands are full."

The labor   This is well under way once we are consistently setting standards and limits that our children object to because they want to do what they want to do. As we persist, they struggle with us. Our mutual struggles enable the labor to progress. The important thing to understand is that only through these joint efforts do they make the necessary emotional transformations. From babies who are dependent on Mommy and Daddy, they turn into relatively self-reliant children who have entered into their families. It takes many hundreds of incidents for them to make the transition.

Think of all those times you had with your two-year-olds in which nothing seemed to satisfy or settle them, when they were not open to doing what you told them. The things about which they were upset were often trivial and simple to us, but not so for them. Our insistence until they complied was, nonetheless, very important:

★ "Put on your shirt, now."

★ "You can have ice-cream after you drink your milk."

★ "Leave your toys there and come here."

The transition   At this stage, our children are almost ready to move from their struggling, passionate ways of living to something much more comfortable for everyone, including themselves. A sign is that they become increasingly settled, cooperative, and willing to do things as and when asked or expected. However, they do still need or seem to need prompting at this stage.

Another sign is that parents often get "the transition blues":

★ "I don't think I can keep this up any longer."

★ "Someone else can do it now, we've done our part."

★ "This will never end."

★ "Everything I do doesn't seem to make any difference."

★ "I just want all of this to stop; I'm tired of struggles."

Interestingly, the more intense these sentiments are, the closer the end generally is. At these times, it helps to remember that "the night is always darkest just before the dawn." And by the way, many women feel similarly at transition during the physical birth.

The delivery   Only repeated contractions produce the labor that leads to the delivery. And with delivery comes great relief. In fact, we know the delivery is completed when we experience sustained relief. Our two-year-olds turn into amenable, available, cooperative, loveable, and, at the same time, assertive, clear-thinking, self-contained little children. As they do, we learn that all those times that we stood our ground have paid off.

Action is imperative

It is important to note that we must act: no contractions, no labor, no delivery. Unlike the physical birth, there are no "emotional caesarians." In other words, unless we stand firm during this time, our children remain emotional babies. You can see this in many older children whose parents did not stand their ground enough. These children continue for years to act like two-year-olds by throwing tantrums or manipulating to get what they want.

A third birth for teenagers

Now we come back to fourteen-year-olds. The point of describing the emotional birth of two-year-olds is that another birth occurs at about fourteen years of age. This one follows the same sequence. Also, while it is a "cognitive birth," it requires very similar persistence and involvement as the emotional birth, except that our children are much older and the issues are usually different.

The cognitive birth of the teenager   At about thirteen, teenagers revisit their baby years (see Chapters 4 and 15). At about fourteen, they revisit the two-year-old period. So part of what they are doing at this age is reworking their second birth—the emotional one. At the same time, however, they are also going through a third birth— a cognitive one. They have lots to cope with!

The start   The birth begins with resistance again, with arguments and "picking fights" over all sorts of things. The objections often relate to who knows what, who decides what is real, and how to take control of all of that. For example:

★ "Leave me alone! What do you know?!"

★ "You can't make me do it. Just try, you'll see!"

★ "What a stupid idea! Why would you want to do that?"

★ "You don't know what you're talking about!"

★ "You don't understand anything!"

Our teenagers often seem to have become wilfully determined to make life as uncomfortable as they can.

The contractions   As with two-year-olds, we create contractions when we, or other adults like their teachers, stand firm with them. We do this over a variety of daily issues. We might, for example:

★ insist on courtesy and respect for everyone

★ set standards and limits, and apply rewards and consequences

★ persist in applying consequences for their noncompliance

★ stay engaged, passionately at times, until all issues are resolved.

The labor   As with the previous births, the labor of this birth involves repeated contractions. In other words, we need to persist with our side of the process, day after day, if necessary. We know of two very effective ways of making sure that the labor progresses:

★ Ask fourteen-year-olds to do at least three things a day that they may not want to do. As well as prompting contractions, this means that we get to choose some of what to struggle over.

★ Avoid postponing action and respond every time our fourteen-year-olds act outside the guidelines.

The labor of this birth can take up to a year. Many hundreds of encounters are involved and each one contributes, just like in the physical birth. So it is clear that fourteen-year-olds need our regular, persistent and committed involvement to complete this birth. Also, there is usually no escape. When we try to avoid, sidestep, ignore, or in other ways not respond to their invitations and provocations to struggle, they will usually become increasingly demanding or provocative until we do respond.

Somehow they instinctively know that they need us to stand firmly enough for them to have something strong enough to push against for their births to progress. Their desire to be born into the adult world is profoundly powerful and they keep at us until we play our parts. Fortunately, some of the pressure is also taken by other adults who get roped into the process. Teachers and others in authority are particularly likely to receive these invitations!

The labor is trying

Very few people would claim that this labor is easy, particularly if we are uncomfortable with struggle. So it is natural for us to have many doubts about what we are doing. To add to our "woes," for the process to work, we actually do need to feel uncomfortable at times. It is only when all involved are uncomfortable that lots of teenagers feel connected and engaged enough to progress. This is why they are so very skilled at getting us to feel uncertain, illogical, inconsistent, unreasonable, unfair, and frustrated— sometimes all at once! They need us feeling like this precisely because they are feeling very much the same.

The transition   We reach transition when the young ones are:

★ showing signs of gracefully adapting to our expectations and limits

★ recognizing that doing so is worthwhile and much more comfortable than not

★ increasingly taking the initiative to act as we expect them to act.

The other signal is that we often feel at our wits' end, hopeless about the hassles ever going away, "certain" that no progress has been made in all the months gone by, and other similarly "optimistic" sentiments! Contrary to appearances, however, when feeling this way after months of persistence, we are very close to the end and it is time to remember "the dark of night and the coming dawn" again.

The delivery   Provided we labor effectively, delivery is inevitable. The delivery enables young people to change from being children in the womb of the family to being very young adults ready to bond with the community at large. The delivery is complete when they become sociable, socialized, curious, appealing, helpful, and thinking people.

When they do, it is clear that they have learned to use thinking to help manage themselves and how they act, and no longer to allow their feelings to dominate them. They then enter a stage of learning that is very focused on thinking and its further development, something made possible by the delivery that ends this birth.

Complete delivery depends on adult involvement

Until the end, remember that successful delivery depends on parents and other significant adults playing their parts. Fortunately, some of the load can be shared with others. Remember, too, that there are no caesarians at this age, just like at age two. It is up to us as adult representatives of the community to do what is required. We are the birth canal.

CHAPTER 8

Community involvement

Gerald was in the garage cleaning his tools after a particularly dirty job. Very preoccupied with what he was doing, he was surprised when he became aware that Andrew, his son, had just come up beside him.

"What are you doing, Dad?" he asked curiously.

Anyone else may have taken this at face value, but Gerald was already preparing himself for an argument. During the previous nine months even an innocent question like this could be a lead-in for trouble. "Just cleaning some tools after fixing the engine," he said cautiously.

"Did you get it finished?" Andrew was obviously interested, while Gerald was still holding his breath, waiting for a flare-up.

"Yeah. I've still got a bit more to do this afternoon, though. That's why I'm cleaning these." He raised some greasy spanners for Andrew to see.

Andrew then headed for the door, only to stop midway. "Dad," his voice was clear and open, "would you like me to mow the lawns for you this afternoon? You're busy and I don't have anything much to do."

Gerald's jaw dropped and he just stared. Catching himself after a few seconds, he hastily and enthusiastically said, "I certainly would." Andrew immediately found the mower without assistance and took it outside. As he got on with the mowing, Gerald got on with the cleaning, shaking his head in disbelief from time to time. "What a difference," he said to himself, "I hope this lasts."

The "hidden beauty" in the fourteen-year-old struggles is that they are preparation for better times. "Beauty" is not, of course, a word many parents would use to describe the process while they are in the middle of it! However, the struggles do end and usually end well when we have done most of what our fourteen-year-olds need us to do. In fact, there are many other gains, too, gains that we discuss in Chapter 16.

In this chapter, we describe how fifteen-year-olds are prepared by the labor they have just been through to bond with the adult communities in which they live. We also highlight how important this bonding is and how they need contact with the adults around them to make it possible.

Be aware that these ages are guidelines only. The timing of the bonding is very important. Young people who complete their deliveries before turning fifteen need the bonding opportunities we are about to discuss at that time. So avoid artificially waiting until they turn fifteen before you start, if they are already showing the signs that they are born.

Bonding and birth

Bonding is the final stage of birth. It takes place immediately after the delivery. Interestingly, the very intensity of the contractions is what significantly prepares everyone for the bonding. Without this intensity, bonding is often less powerful and enduring.

Bonding—usually a joyous time

Rapturous love and pleasure often saturate all present—feelings that open us to engage ourselves deeply with the new arrival.

★ *As we unite, we welcome them.*

★ *We put past struggles behind us and celebrate the emergence of the new "baby" in our midst.*

★ *We look forward in anticipation to a wonderful shared future.*

★ *Following a natural urge, we commit to making ourselves available and to providing whatever the new arrival needs to thrive in our midst.*

★ *Our children form a deep sense of belonging with us and the other people with whom they bond at that time.*

Early bonds

Children experience two intense bonding times before their teenage years. Both are very important. The first follows the physical birth at zero years and the second occurs at three years of age after the emotional birth. We explore these here, because they give us many important guidelines on how we need to respond to the fifteen-year-old's need to bond.

Preparation for bonding   The rigors of labor in a normal birth stimulate and ready both the "baby" and the "mother" for their joining at the end. The excitation of the labor combined with the relief that accompanies the delivery produces a potent "glue" capable of bonding them together for life.

Physical preparation   During the physical birth, the muscular contractions create strong physical responses in both mother and baby. The physical tension of each contraction clearly impacts the mother. What is less often understood is that the contractions stimulate the baby too. Also, both mother and baby are further stimulated by the pressures and tensions that result from the baby being squeezed down the birth canal and then through the vaginal opening. So, at the delivery, the bodies of both are in a high state of excitation.

Emotional preparation   During the emotional birth, the stimulation comes from the emotional struggles. The "mother" is the family as a whole. Mothers, fathers, brothers, sisters, or any other people who are regularly present, all play a part. The family could be a single mother or father, or parents who have no other children. Boarders and regular visitors are included. The family is made up of all those people who engage with the child on a fairly regular basis at home. Everyone generally finds two-year-old demands, passions, and tantrums highly stimulating, even those who are only spectators. The two-year-olds themselves are already highly charged because of the intensity of their feelings. So by the time months of struggle have passed and the delivery is imminent, most people present are in a state of high emotional arousal.

The bonding itself   Bonding occurs through intense exchanges between "mother" and "baby" during the crucial time immediately after the delivery.

Physical bonding   When the newborn baby is given to the mother the physical bonding occurs. Suckling, holding, eye contact, and talking are generally all-important parts of this. The most powerful physical connections are established in the first few hours after the birth. The closer to the delivery the bonding occurs, the more powerful it is. Very importantly, fathers and others present can also bond during this time.

Emotional bonding   This occurs when the "newborn child," usually about three years of age, is taken into the bosom of the family,

The physical bond of the first birth forms a primary foundation for all later intimate relationships. It makes possible the deep sense of connectedness that is fundamental to those relationships.

welcomed, cherished, and loved there. The relief produced for all by the "cessation of hostilities" has a profound impact and fuels the desire to form a very different and loving relationship.

We help to form these emotional bonds when we lovingly and joyously tell children that they are important members of our families, give them special jobs to do that contribute meaningfully to others, offer them special privileges and help them to find their place as family members. A special meal or other celebration helps to add to the festive nature of what is occurring. The closer all this is to when the two-year-old struggles end, the more strongly children will bond emotionally with their families.

The emotional bonds of the second birth form a significant foundation for emotional openness and connectedness. They enable people to relate to others and exchange meaningfully and intimately with each other through their feelings.

Who to bond with

You have probably seen photos or movies of ducklings following human beings, kittens following dogs, even animals following wheelbarrows around.

We were once told about a failed attempt at breeding two female dogs, which had been very keen to fulfill their desire. The male dog selected for the job actually ran away from their amorous advances. Unfortunately for the females, the dog did not know he was a dog. He thought he was a cat because he had been orphaned as a newborn and put to a mother cat, which suckled and raised him.

The point of these examples is very important. Almost without exception, newborns bond with what is waiting for them at their births. All that needs to happen is for the newborn to spot something and to seek contact with it. It also helps for that something at least to seem to respond. So, for example, a moving wheelbarrow is likely to attract more attention than a stationary one!

The same is true of human beings. We bond with whomever or whatever is there and available to us. So it is very important that those who are to be responsible for nurturing a newborn are available to bond—and at the right time. Remember, timing is crucial. Missing the appointment has very serious consequences.

Babies bond with parents
Babies need to bond physically with their mothers, in particular, and with their fathers. As a bonus, babies may also bond with brothers and sisters, or other close relatives, if they are there.

Obviously, it is important for the baby to be given to its parents immediately after the birth so the strongest possible bonds are formed. Consequently, routine and unnecessary medical procedures are best postponed until after bonding has occurred, or the baby will attempt to bond with the medical personnel handling them and the implements they are using. Clearly, when a baby needs medical intervention to preserve its life or to avert some serious physical problems, these need to take priority. Or if the mother is unavailable for some reason, say she is anesthetized, or the father cannot be present, then the bonding will not be possible with them. Even so, it is important to have as much intense contact with our children as soon as possible after their birth so we can bond strongly with them.

Three-year-olds bond with families
Three-year-olds need to bond emotionally with their families. So their families—mothers, fathers, and other members—need to make themselves available for this. If they are not there, then the bonding cannot occur with them and will occur with whomever or whatever is around. For example, our three-year-olds may bond emotionally with their childcare providers rather than with us. We may then wonder why we don't feel as emotionally close to them as we did before. Also, they may feel emotionally cut off from us and not part of the family in which they are living.

Teenage bonding

Let's now turn to teenage bonding. This occurs immediately after the cognitive birth. The "mother" is the community of people around the teenager at the time. It is this community of people that needs to stand ready to receive the teenage "newborn" when they arrive.

The preparation   Our passionate exchanges with fourteen-year-olds produce the necessary stimulation in everyone that primes us all for the bonding to come. After up to a year of contractions, everyone is usually more than ready to come together with relief, pleasure, love, joy, and sharing when the labor stops.

The bonding   Fifteen-year-olds ideally bond with the grown-up communities in which they will live from then on. To do this, they need representatives of their communities to accept them and give them heartfelt welcome, as part of inducting them into the adult life of those communities. Usually parents, teachers, employers, and other adults involved with the teenagers are enlisted to play their parts.

The window of opportunity to do this is relatively limited, so we need to stay alert for when to act. The best time to act is immediately following their shift to significantly more cooperative and friendly ways of living. We need to strike while the teenagers are cool!

What adults need to offer fifteen-year-olds

★   *ways to understand their lives in the community context in which they live*

★   *knowledge and information about community life, values, and expectations*

★   *discussion of how to live well*

★   *ideas on the kinds of things that are and are not valued*

★   *opportunities to experiment with all of this*

★   *specific ways to contribute to those around them.*

Bonding in tribal groups   In many tribal cultures, at around the age of thirteen to fifteen, the men took over the boys and the women took over the girls. By about fifteen years of age their initiations into adulthood had been conducted. Special rites were practiced, involving clear, public displays that marked the transition from childhood to adulthood. The adults in the community made these displays to say very clearly, "We are welcoming you and this is what we are welcoming you into." All this activity made it abundantly clear whom they were to bond with, and adults went to great lengths to connect and strengthen the bonds.

It is interesting that in many groups these rites of passage started at the age of about thirteen, when teenagers are most impressionable, and carried on through the following two years. Seen from the perspective we are presenting here, these rites were very much to do with assisting the transition from the confined world of children who lived with their families to the adult world that was the support of the family as a whole.

Modern bonding opportunities   By contrast, our communities as whole units generally do not do anything significant to encourage teenagers to bond with them. This is a big gap in what is offered to the young these days. Without ways of bonding to their communities, these bond-hungry young people cannot develop the healthy sense of belonging that they need.

At the same time, many groups within our communities do offer opportunities. For example, Jewish people have Bar Mitzvah celebrations for boys and Bat Mitzvah celebrations for girls; some Christian denominations have confirmation. Some schools, and other groups like the Scouts, fulfill this function well. Each gradually inducts its members into their group, teaching teenagers the values, approaches, and other aspects of how to be a contributing member of the group and of the wider community.

Teenage bonding alternatives

Parents and adults with an interest in the young need to understand that our availability is crucial. When we are unavailable, we force our teenagers to look elsewhere. Remember, they have a profound need to bond and they will. Also, they will bond with whoever is there for them. If we are, they will bond with us. If we are not, they will bond with those who are.

> ### Ways parents/adults show their unavailability
>
> ★ *"busyness" at work*
>
> ★ *not making opportunities to spend time with teenagers*
>
> ★ *pulling back with the intent of giving space*
>
> ★ *feeling resentful over the previous year or years of struggle*
>
> ★ *showing a lack of interest*
>
> ★ *acting out their feelings of inadequacy*
>
> ★ *rejecting their teenagers.*

Other adults   In our absence, and if they are fortunate, then interested adults outside our families will make themselves available to them. In fact, many teenagers actively seek out and latch onto the parents of friends, adults at school, sports coaches, Scout or Guide leaders, youth workers, or others.

Their peers   In the absence of any adults, teenagers usually turn to their peers, with whom other powerful forces act in addition to their basic needs for bonding. So there is a lot to attract and hold them:

★ Many teenagers are in rebellion against adults and they feel supported in this by others who are too.

★ Peer groups often show clearly who is "in" and who is "out."

★ Peer groups offer teenagers an intensity of contact, involvement, and excitement that is often unavailable elsewhere.

★ Teenage groups often have codes of behavior that govern how to act with members and with non-members.

Adults who attract the young

These adults generally:

★   *are readily accessible*

★   *value them as people*

★   *encourage involvement and contact*

★   *enjoy discussion and other exchanges with them*

★   *relish initiating them into a grown-up understanding of the community.*

Understandably, then, when adrift at home or in the adult world, lots of teenagers feel they belong with their peers. And when together, they may act in ways that highlight their connectedness and the power of that. Think of how they are in public, for example.

We see them gathering on street corners, leaning against shop fronts, walking in groups along the pavement, or hogging the space at bus shelters. While much of what they do is good-natured and benign, many teenagers go through a phase of liking to intimidate adults and other children. They do it with their size and numbers, with aggressive manners, and with acting in ways that challenge usual public standards. Most soften these activities as they learn to manage their growing bodies and personal power. Others get hooked on the power and continue to enjoy the results of their bullying.

Peer groups with definite cultures offer the chance to belong to a body of people with a definite identity and "strength in numbers." This is a heady brew for many uncertain youngsters who are in search of a place to belong.

What we can do

We offer several guidelines. All aim to ensure that fifteen-year-olds bond with the communities in which they live and learn to belong in the adult world around them. We recommend that parents:

★ ensure that they physically spend time with them when they are ready to bond

★ engage intensely and often enough with them to ensure that their bonds and sense of belonging can develop

★ introduce their teenagers to other adults and to groups whose members will provide good guidance and role models

★ monitor what is happening to ensure that everything is fine.

To foster an extended community commitment to the next generation, we are sure that other adult members of the community also need to act. As adults we need to:

★ make ourselves available to teenagers as formal or informal mentors

★ stay aware of what young people are doing and do something if they seem to be in trouble

★ report unruly, unlawful, dangerous, or threatening behavior to authorities as quickly as possible to interrupt it

★ let other parents know if their children seem to be in or creating trouble, or are doing well, acting responsibly, or enjoying themselves

★ support other adults who are acting responsibly with their own or other people's teenagers

★ be prepared to support friends and acquaintances, when asked, to form groups of adults who take a combined or individual stand on "right living" with teenagers who are deviating too much from the appropriate path.

Important
issues

This section has special meaning. It addresses

significant issues that have arisen repeatedly in our

contact with parents. These issues include the

fundamental importance of parents, the need for us to

stay involved with our teenagers, and what to do if they

try to manipulate or control us. The emphasis

throughout is on how to manage ourselves while we do

what is necessary to manage, nurture, and protect our

young. The perspectives offered and the practical

suggestions made are intended to bring

understanding—even joy—to our relationships with our

teenagers and to secure the best outcomes for them.

CHAPTER 9

Staying engaged with your teenager

We live at a time when a great deal is known about raising children. The information is widely available. Admittedly, when we start to look into it, we find a great variety of opinions, many of which conflict. So we have some sorting to do.

In this chapter, we briefly explore six areas, each containing important background to, or guidelines for, raising teenagers well.

The place of parents

The basic connection between parents and children is biological. At the same time, there is much more going on than biology. Deep-rooted psychological connections are also in play. These help to hold parents and children together throughout the 21 years that fully raising a child takes. So powerful are these binding forces that it takes the full 21 years to loosen them naturally. Importantly, rupturing parent-child bonds prematurely is profoundly disturbing for the young.

Human young rely on their parents to feed, shelter, nurture, train and, when they are ready, to launch them into the world. This has been true for however many years—hundreds of thousands or millions— human beings have lived on this planet. And it is naïve for us to imagine, as some do, that a few brief years of modern living have significantly altered such deeply ingrained needs and processes.

Our children need us. They need us for 21 years. When we are there for them, they can and usually will do very well, although there are no guarantees of safety and well-being, even then. By contrast, we can almost guarantee that not being there for them puts their safety and well-being significantly at risk.

Engagement, safety, and well-being

Given their need for their parents, it is little wonder that the safest, least at-risk teenagers are usually well engaged with their parents. Having a stable family base is a wonderful asset for teenagers going through turbulent times. It makes a huge difference when they know that at least one person cares, values them, and is interested in them.

Importantly, being engaged with someone in this way is proven to reduce the risk of suicide and depression in teenagers. Clearly our teenagers seem to know what they need, too, because in the absence of someone at home they often seek someone outside.

Engagement has to do with involvement, showing them that they matter to us and being there to support, help, and guide when they need it. While not always welcomed, and maybe even spurned at times, our involvement is crucial. Remember, as pointed out in Chapter 3, struggle is both normal and necessary in teenagers and is not, in itself, a sign that we are making mistakes.

Ways parents can stay well engaged with teenagers

★ *Spend time with them regularly day after day.*

★ *Have evening meals together on most nights.*

★ *Show an interest in them as people.*

★ *Use opportunities to hang out with them at home or elsewhere.*

★ *Take an interest in what they do.*

★ *Do housework together.*

★ *Keep track of them by knowing where they are and what they are doing.*

★ *Express feelings and passions to each other.*

★ *Discuss issues, thoughts, and feelings.*

★ *Offer clear guidance and limits, and set consequences.*

★ *Present and discuss adult values and ethics with them.*

Truly knowing our teenagers

Teenagers do much better when they sense that we understand them. Interestingly, this does not require that we agree with them, or that we allow them to do what they like when they like. It has to do with their experiencing that we understand their side of things, that we see who they are, that we hear what they are saying, and that we feel what is important to them.

Particularly when pushed, lots of parents start to act as if they understand their children better than they do. They do not act with respect for their young:

★ "I know what you're thinking."

★ "You don't have to tell me what you were up to, I know."

★ "Listen to me, I know what is going on with you."

We truly respect and are more likely to know our children when we seek their side of things directly from them. This requires that we be alert to them, their feelings, their needs, their interests and priorities, their hopes and dreams—their ways of understanding themselves and what is going on around them. We need to find out these things *from them*, if we are to honor them. And the simplest thing to do is to ask them directly.

Importantly, "finding out" is not the same as agreeing, supporting, or going along with them. The point is to understand them, because to engage them in life, as we understand it, we need to start with where they are. (You will find many useful ways of communicating with your teenagers in Chapters 13 to 16 of *ParentCraft*. We highly recommend that you read these chapters and use what you think will help.)

Discipline—standards and limits

Increasingly often these days, experts are urging parents of teenagers to use discipline. This is something of a change from the practices common during the last few decades. The point of recommending discipline is to strengthen the young and to free them. A seeming contradiction to some adults, this recommendation makes complete sense when understood. People who can manage themselves with disciplined confidence are usually more likely to make sensible decisions—both during serious times and during times of fun. Also, they are more likely to achieve what is important to them.

Teenagers absorb from us what we have to do to manage them and, with our repetition, they learn to use our approaches internally for themselves.

Teenagers are often in the grip of very strong feelings; they are also learning many new skills and are having to handle rapidly expanding worlds. As we manage and guide them while they do all of this, we teach them how to manage themselves. Our effectiveness becomes theirs.

The discipline sequence

Five simple steps help us to teach discipline day by day:

1   **Expectations** *Say what standards we expect of them and what we are limiting them from doing. From this, they know what to do and what not to do. Both aspects are important.*

2   **Reasons** *Outline why we expect what we do. Giving our reasons invites them to think about things for themselves and to act rationally.*

3   **Consequences** *Set consequences for compliance and noncompliance. Make sure we only choose things we are prepared to do. Also, what we choose needs to matter to our teenagers.*

4   **Agreements** *Get agreements from them about the future. This is a crucial step, because it carries their learning on into the future. Without it, learning is usually very much slower.*

5   **Follow-up** *Ensure that we get what we expect. If we follow up, our teenagers know that we mean what we say. If not, they are likely to stop taking much notice of what we expect of them and, in the end, of what they expect of themselves.*

Here is an example:

Your daughter is unreliable about doing her homework and wants to go out instead. (*Expectations*) "I expect you to do your homework before you go out tonight. You are not to postpone it until later." (*Reasons*) "Doing your homework regularly will make school easier and more enjoyable. At the moment, you're getting behind and that's already making school more difficult." (*Consequences*) "After you've done your homework, you can go out immediately. If you don't do it now, you'll stay here and not go out." (*Agreement*) "Do you agree to do your homework now?" (Of course, she agrees immediately!) (*Follow-up*) After allowing enough time, you check on progress and apply the consequences as outlined. For the future, you keep applying the same principles to her doing her homework.

Useful things to remember

★ *Learning discipline takes years.*

★ *Getting well engaged helps.*

★ *Consistency is very important.*

★ *Inconsistency makes us seem unreliable and unsafe.*

★ *Follow-up is imperative.*

★ *Teenagers are pushing the limits to get us to stand our ground.*

Life's lessons

The lessons we learn most strongly are the ones that come from what we do in life. Sometimes parents act as if all they have to do is tell their teenagers what to do and that is enough. Very often, however, it is not. They need to experience the consequences of doing or not doing things before our "lessons" become truly meaningful to them.

Aaron, at sixteen, was still very unreliable with time. Often late, he seemed oblivious to the frustration and inconvenience he caused others. After repeated failed attempts to get him to understand, his parents made a plan. He loved going swimming and was very good at it, so they decided to make him late next time he wanted to go. Soon enough a swimming meet was announced. Aaron was to be there at 1:30 p.m. and they, like he usually did, agreed to be on time. However, on the day, they held him up by doing many of the sorts of things Aaron usually did with them. On arriving late, he had to deal with his angry coach and teammates. The next time he was late, his parents quietly reminded him of how he felt about the swimming meet. He was punctual from then on.

Resilience and coping

Resilience is a real asset for teenagers. It is the capacity to recover or bounce back from setbacks. Resilient young people have a buoyancy in their responses that helps them to keep facing the challenges of their lives until they are successful.

If we look at teenagers generally, we find that some are more resilient than others. Understandably, what we also find is that the ones who cope best with their lives are generally the most resilient. So what can we do, if our teenagers are not very resilient?

Fortunately, our resilience with them helps them to develop resilience of their own. In other words, at least to some extent, they can learn it from us. The main thing is for us to set good examples.

Teaching and supporting resilience

★ *Persist in getting them to face what is happening.*

★ *Keep coming back for more, whatever they do to put us off.*

★ *Continue to deal with our own issues.*

★ *Notice what works and learn from mistakes.*

★ *Consistently celebrate their successes and enjoy their lives.*

★ *Avoid holding grudges, even if they are unpleasant.*

★ *Keep looking for solutions—don't give up, even if pushed.*

★ *Seek solutions and fulfillment in every situation.*

CHAPTER 10

Hostage parents

"Here is the news . . .

"This is Kitty Close of U2 TV. In the home behind me an unknown teenage boy has taken a woman and two children hostage. He is believed to be holding them at gunpoint. Already shots have been fired at the police, who arrived on the scene thirty minutes ago. Police negotiators are in contact with the boy as I speak. His demands are not yet known to us, but we will let you know when we get some news. Meanwhile, back to the studio."

While this scenario may seem far-fetched to you, it is regrettably very common in many homes. Fortunately, only a few involve life-threatening situations. However, the tyranny by young people of their parents is a daily experience in many families. Some mothers and fathers feel powerless to stand their ground in the face of the threatening demands and manipulations made by their teenage children. And they give in.

This chapter is particularly for those parents who have to deal with moderate to serious behavior at home—parents whose teenage children have virtually taken them over. It contains useful suggestions on how to get free and to assert the authority we as parents need to exercise for everyone's welfare and safety.

In reality, the suggestions also apply to many families with younger children. Lots of parents give up their power and authority long before their children become teenagers. So, while we are describing teenagers here, what we are saying is directly relevant to many families with younger children, too.

Hostages in the home

"But our children don't threaten to shoot anyone," some parents say when first introduced to this idea. And for these parents this is probably true. However, young people have many other techniques that are as effective. And in the families concerned there is no doubt that the parents are hostage to their teenagers. The parents, who are the supposed authorities in the home, are meant to manage all family members. However, not wanting this, the teenagers keep threatening their parents until they get their own way. During the process, any attempts by parents to achieve compliance with their expectations are met with escalating threats.

Techniques of the young   Many young people are very skilled at using emotional, psychological, and social weapons to get what they want. They do not need to resort to physical weapons or physical abuse, precisely because the other ones work so well.

Ways of holding parents hostage

★ wrong-footing us by looking, sounding, or acting in just the "right way": snarling, sneering, condescending, accusing, ignoring, pouting, suffering, whining, raging . . .

★ menacing or intimidating us with their physical size by moving up too close, puffing themselves up physically as if about to "explode," making or shaking fists, glaring belligerently . . .

★ shouting threats, abuse, or insults

★ making a public spectacle of themselves or us

★ physically or verbally assaulting us

★ threatening to do or actually doing things that will worry us enormously: running away from home, staying out until all hours, taking drugs, breaking the law . . .

★ acting in rejecting, withdrawing ways: not talking, running out of the room or house, going coldly silent or forbidding ...

Also, the young are usually very selective, which is to be expected when we think about it. Our teenagers have known us for a long time, so they know just the right buttons to press to hold us captive until we give up and give them what they want. Of course, many young people would never dream of acting like this with their parents. This unfortunately is beside the point, for those who do are usually motivated very differently.

Teenage motivation   The teenagers who are inclined to go to extremes want control and will do what it takes to get it. Their parents need to understand this. Whatever these teenagers do, at the time they are doing it they are almost always convinced that they are completely justified in doing so. Implacability and ruthless lack of sensitivity to others are key aspects of the behavior of such teenagers. This style of behavior is particularly challenging to parents, as they are also having to face the difficult reality of their children acting like this at all.

Put briefly, then, lots of teenagers do not need to resort to the use of physical weapons or physical abuse to get what they want. Mind you, as mentioned, such acts or threats are a regular part of the lives of many parents.

> Frederica was a single mother with a physical disability that meant she had to use crutches to get around. Ilse, her tall and heavy fourteen-year-old daughter, often physically attacked her to get her own way. At different times, she had hit her, pushed her over, or beat her with one of her crutches. Often she had physically menaced her as she shouted abuse. As a result, Frederica would, for example, unnecessarily spend the rent money on the latest fad shoes or clothing that her daughter wanted. Frederica felt completely powerless with this out-of-control young person.

Teenagers choose the weapons they do precisely because they work. And they work because parents give control of themselves or their families over to their teenagers. The result is a hostage situation in which the teenagers run the show, using all sorts of techniques of intimidation or coercion to do it.

Why the techniques work   None of the techniques of these teenagers would work if we parents were prepared to "face them down," were sure that we could do so safely, were confident about the outcomes, and could manage our feelings and other responses as we did what was necessary. However, for many parents of coercive teenagers, this is easier to say than to do.

Common reasons parents don't stand up to teenagers

★   *We are afraid of getting hurt, or that others will get hurt.*

★   *We don't like our children not liking us.*

★   *We feel completely stuck and don't know how to get free.*

★   *We worry about what others will think if we make a fuss.*

★   *We blame ourselves if our children get into trouble.*

★   *We think we will lose control if we start to act strongly.*

★   *We made unhelpful decisions when we were young: never, for example, to interfere, or to stop our children getting what they want.*

The inhibiting power of our responses has a lot to do with their origins in the past. Usually our patterns started early in our lives, and were reinforced time and again as we grew up. It is little wonder, then, that we find parenting our teenagers challenging. Perhaps we can take some comfort from knowing that lots of others are struggling as we are, but we need to do more than this. *We need to learn to deal with what is going on.*

Freeing the hostages

"*Now, back to the news . . .*

"This is Kitty Close again from U2 TV. The good news from here is that the hostages were released a few moments ago. Clearly upset but relieved to be free, they were ushered away from the house. It seems that a police officer was able to keep the hostage-taker talking and persuade him to hand himself over to the officer. In fact, standing with me is Captain Freeman who's been in charge here tonight. Captain, will you tell us how you handled this?"

"Thank you, Kitty. Yes, well obviously the most important thing was to free the hostages with a minimum of trouble. Usually the best thing to do is to wait actively. This is what we did. We kept talking, making it clear that we couldn't give him what he wanted. On a couple of occasions, he started to act dangerously, so we offered to make a concession or two, but we always asked for a concession from him at the same time. The aim throughout was to keep extending the time. What we've found is that, as time passes, hostage-takers usually start to realize the reality of their situation: 'I might want to get away with this, but I won't actually be able to.' When all goes well, hostage-takers give up in the end, release the hostages, and place themselves in the hands of the authorities. I'm delighted that this was the outcome tonight."

"Was there ever any danger to the hostages, Captain?"

"Well, once or twice we were getting worried. We were prepared to *intervene with force*, but fortunately we didn't have to here. If we had, the objective would have been to overcome the hostage-taker and release his captives. Of course, where physical violence is threatened or used against hostages, for direct action to work there are serious risks that have to be dealt with. Unfortunately, at times, hostage-takers are so fixed on winning their demands that nothing else matters to them. Decisive action is then required. I'm only glad that it wasn't needed here."

How parents get free

★ Hold on to what is important *in the face of all threats and manipulations. Say: "You are to do . . . You are not to do . . . and what you are doing now doesn't change that."*

★ Keep going, *even if the process takes a long time: hours, days, weeks, or months—even years, if necessary!*

★ Repeatedly present the reality of the situation: *"The situation is . . .," "The consequences will be . . .," "Other people will respond by . . .," "You will have to deal with . . . ."*

★ When lives or property are significantly threatened, find ways to take over—*and do it by force if necessary: call the police, get a Crisis Assessment Team on the job, get friends in to help, arrange an Intervention Order at the court.*

Strategies from parents who cope well

★ Continue to hold on to what you know is right.

★ Have clear ideas of the outcomes you want for your teenagers: *live at home, study well at school, have friends . . .*

★ Have definite expectations about how your children should behave: *talk politely, take account of others and themselves, discuss problems without resorting to "power plays" . . .*

★ Have a sense of inner strength, or get support from others to do what you know is important: *"I can do this and I need to for his/her sake," "When I need help, I'll call . . . ."*

★ Have tolerance for the discomfort you feel when your children don't like something: *anguish, fear, anger, worry, guilt . . .*

★ Make a commitment to deal effectively with what is happening, no matter what: *"I will do what is necessary, whatever it takes; I will find out how to do it if I don't know, and I will practice until I succeed."*

Learning the ropes   "All right," you may think, "but if I could do all of that, I wouldn't have a problem." And, of course, that is true. So what can we do to learn? Let's take them in order:

1   *Decide the outcomes you want.* Discuss with your co-parent and other adults directly involved what your teenagers are doing. Clarify the outcomes you want. It is much easier to act with determination when we know what we are aiming at. Books like *ParentCraft* and *Adolescence: A guide for parents* can help, as they contain all sorts of ideas about achievable outcomes.

2   *Decide on how you want your teenagers to act.* Discuss with your co-parent and other involved adults what is desirable behavior and what is unacceptable behavior. Having these clear enables us to concentrate on the behavior we want and on what we expect our teenagers to avoid. Both are important. Also, if our teenagers favor bullying tactics, we can get all sorts of strategies from a wonderful book called *Bully Busting* by Evelyn Field.

3   *Build your inner strength and external support systems.* If you have little self-confidence, then consider getting professional help to develop it. Many skilled practitioners are available these days. Options include everything from good parenting classes to counselors and psychotherapists.

    In addition, enlist the help of other adults as a support system. Then, when your teenagers start to use power tactics to ignore, coerce, or manipulate you, and remain unresponsive to your efforts, call in the backup team. This evens up the situation. If what you are dealing with is dangerous, you will need to make sure that the people you involve are aware of the dangers and are prepared to deal with them. Details of two very informative books on what is called "tough love" are included in "Authors' notes" at the back of this book. Many parents find these very helpful.

4   *Develop tolerance for creating discomfort in others.* You can also seek professional help to learn this. Importantly, the purpose is not to become callous; it is to develop the strength to pull out the "emotional splinters" our teenagers get at times. We must pull them out, even when it "hurts," or they will have problems later. Practice by showing them who is in control on simple things:

★ Comment on small things you do and don't like (both are important).

★ Ask them to do at least three very small things for you each day.

★ Interrupt and get their attention briefly when they are engrossed in something else.

5   *Make a commitment to do whatever is required.* Having the desire to do what is needed, even a very strong desire, is often not enough. Feelings and desires change like the wind. You need to commit to doing what is necessary. This stabilizes things and makes it much easier to act. "I will get my son to listen to me tonight and I will keep him up until he does" is very different from "I really want to get my son to take notice of me and I hope I'll manage." We can use this difference very powerfully.

To help your confidence and resolve, read on!

CHAPTER **11**
The big secret

The "big secret" is probably the best kept secret in childhood. Generation after generation of teenagers seem to manage to keep it from their parents. Then, astoundingly, when they become parents in their turn, they forget it. By doing so, they put themselves through much more anguish and worry than they would if they had remembered it.

The secret is: teenagers want us (their parents and other adults) to succeed in managing, guiding, teaching, protecting, nurturing, and supporting them, no matter how much they pretend otherwise.

Their stated position is "I don't need you or want you." Their actual position is "I need you, but won't let on."

With this secret revealed, you have a treasure beyond price. Its riches can "buy" you confidence and hope, particularly when your spirits lag in the face of persistent struggle and dissent. It can also act as a beacon to light your way to the end of the teenage journey, even through its darkest times. All you need to do is to remember it and to act on it.

> When she was 24 years of age, Glenda told Frieda, her mother, that she was often offered drugs at school. "Most of my friends used, but I didn't. I always said, 'No.' I could feel you and Dad inside me. I guess I used you as my excuse." "We thought you hated what we were doing," said Frieda. "Well, yes. I felt you were far too strict with me then and I rebelled—a lot." "I remember," Frieda smiled wryly. "But, actually, deep inside I knew you were right," replied Glenda. "And I was so relieved that you were being strict. It kept me out of trouble. Also, I always knew I could turn to you if I was in trouble. Many of my friends didn't feel that about their parents, even though they had much more freedom."

This kind of story is repeated time and again, often when young people reach their early to middle twenties. It is at about this age that they seem to want to come clean as a way of saying "thank you" and, perhaps, as a kind of belated apology to us.

They declare that our persistence and consistency, the limits we set, our willingness to follow up on them, and our determination to see things through to the end were all very important. So from their own mouths, we finally discover that the very actions that produced such outcry at the time were in fact producing wonderful results. Because of what we did, they developed a far greater sense of security and cemented their trust in us far more than if we had been as permissive and as accepting as they demanded at the time.

Understandably, after the event, many parents think, "If only we had known this at the time." They realize rightly that they would have been much more confident and forthright about what they were doing.

Fortunately, you can now do what they regret not doing. You know the secret. You do not have to wait. So act on it confidently!

The message to parents is "Persist and the rewards will come—eventually."

Some years ago, the news ran a report of a fourteen-year-old boy who had succeeded in "divorcing his parents" through the courts. The parents were shown as distraught and unable to comprehend why the law was placing itself between them and their son. They were loving parents whose expectations were completely appropriate. About eight years later, the same boy, now a young man, recanted on the same program. He said that he should never have been allowed by the court to succeed. His parents had been right and he had been wrong. All had suffered.

Reasons why some teenagers struggle for so long

★ *The "uncool virus" infects teenagers and parents.*

★ *Many teenagers regress and it takes time for them to grow up again emotionally.*

★ *The struggles create the contractions of the cognitive birth, a process that can last for the best part of a year.*

★ *Repetition is a normal part of learning and is needed in the reprogramming of the brain that takes them until their early twenties to complete.*

★ *Teenagers learn resilience from our persistence in helping them manage the daily challenges of their lives. This learning involves repeated exposure to our resiliency with them.*

★ *They develop basic trust in us mainly because we engage with them at the times that they need us to be involved— every day, day after day!*

★ *There is a lot for them to learn in the seven years from thirteen to twenty years of age.*

The value of resistance

When teenagers resist us, they strengthen the hold what we say has on them very much more than if they cooperated with us. In fact, the hold on them is as powerful as their resistance. While the opposite of what they and many of us expect, nevertheless it is true. Also, teenagers mostly resist us when they have a particular need to take in strengthened versions of our ways of managing them. They can then manage themselves with the same levels of persistence and strength. So their resistance is an important ally here.

Celebrate resistance! It works for us as parents.

CHAPTER 12

Safety first

Jimmy's parents were talking with the school counselor. They were still reeling after the devastating news a few days earlier that their teenage son had committed suicide. Every exchange was filled with excruciating pain and anguish and the building anger and recriminations that only those who have been through it know.

Mother to the father (crying): "Jimmy's life was falling apart and I didn't even know."

Father to the mother (stiffly): "He was really good at hiding his feelings."

Mother in reply: "But I tried to talk to you about it. Somehow I suspected something. (Her anger was building.) You just didn't want to know. You were so caught up in your work and other things."

Counselor to them both: "I only saw him once, but he wasn't suicidal then. Many teenagers feel the way he did. He was finding it hard to deal with the pressures of school, the demands of sports, and coping with things at home. He did mention that he was having difficulty talking to you two."

Mother: "We would have talked. Why didn't he tell us? It breaks my heart to think he was suffering so much."

Tragically, Jimmy's parents had become too preoccupied with their own immediate interests and concerns: going to their jobs, coping with the housework, arbitrating between children, ferrying them to sports events and other school activities, and managing the family finances. In doing so, they lost contact with Jimmy, who was sending no signals that they noticed of the trouble he was in. Yet, investigation showed that he was sending signals that could have been noticed had the adults around him stayed more alert.

Children in too many families get into trouble because parents miss what is important. Most families *are* loving. We value our children and want the best for them. But some of our children still get into trouble.

Realistically, at times, we can do no more to prevent the problems. Often, however, we can do very much more, and it would make a difference. To do so, of course, we need to recognize the signs and to act on them.

We give some clear information on how to do this in this chapter.

> ## *Staying alert is important*
>
> *In the midst of our "busyness," several things are crucial. We need to:*
>
> ★   *always stay aware of what our young are doing*
>
> ★   *always think about the safety implications of their plans*
>
> ★   *always act decisively and effectively when they are at risk.*

The risks

Our choice of example is deliberately extreme. The reality is that most teenagers are not going to die or get seriously injured. However, the fact is that far too many do. Teenagers are living through a high-risk period in their lives. In the midst of this, they frequently don't know the implications of what they are doing. The distance between life and death in many situations is very small, far too small for us to assume safety and well-being.

For example, serious consequences can flow from a moment of inattention in a dangerous situation, an ill-considered decision to have unprotected sex, an unwise choice to take drugs—all can have life and death consequences. Or the gradual and significant building of difficulties as day follows day may result in our young no longer coping and doing something drastic to remove themselves or to attract our attention to their problems.

Our job as parents is to know what our teenagers are doing and to make sure that they are as protected and as safe as we can.

Keeping teenagers safe

Teenagers need increasing freedom with increasing age. At the same time, parents have the job of keeping them safe. And managing these two important demands is not easy for many of us.

Were we able to control them fully, teenagers might be a lot safer than they are. However, we are not, nor is it wise for us to try. And most parents know both these things. Teenagers do need to venture out into the world where we can no longer control what they do enough to ensure their safety. They need increasingly to spread their wings, because doing so is necessary if they are to learn how to cope with the adult world. Two measures can assist us in helping them to do this safely.

Two safety guidelines

1 *Expand their freedom gradually and only when they are managing how much they already have*. Doing this effectively relies on our having an accurate understanding of each of our teenagers' actual capacities. *To know these, we need to know them well*. So obviously we need to keep in contact with them to achieve this. It also helps for us to have a general idea of what we can expect from teenagers of the ages our teenagers are. To help with this, some precise and general age-specific information on this is available in Section III.

2 *Stay alert and continually do safety-risk assessments*. To do these well for each event, we need to know things such as:

   ★ generally, what they are going to do

   ★ what specific activities are planned

   ★ how safe/dangerous is the plan

   ★ where are they going

   ★ who else will be there

   ★ what supervision, if any, is involved

   ★ who is meeting them

   ★ who is bringing them home

   ★ what time they expect to be back.

We are wise not to assume that everything is safe just because, for example, the school or a parent we know is involved. Not everyone takes safety issues seriously enough for us to count on them, so direct contact with any adults involved is always a good idea.

Do what is necessary

We need to keep doing safety-risk assessments, even if our teenagers think that we are interfering. Far better that they come home safely to challenge us for our "over-concern," than that we have to attend to them at the hospital, police station, or morgue. Besides, the more often we go through the process with them, the more they will learn to think in the same way about safety issues for themselves.

The Rainbow Alert Scale

Of course, in all this, it is crucial to have effective ways of making safety-risk assessments. The Rainbow Alert Scale is designed to help parents and other adults to do so as reliably as possible. It helps us to make the assessments, to decide how urgent action is, and to figure out what to do.

A very important point to make here is that young people can very easily end up dead. Obviously acute risk is important to assess, but assessing chronic escalating risk is also extremely important. In relation to chronic risk, the United States has one of the highest youth suicide rates in the world. It is the third leading cause of death among young adults, with marked increases in recent years. Of course, one person is too many. However, these figures indicate that we have a very significant social problem. We also have a very significant level of youth depression and homelessness.

The Rainbow Alert Scale passes from Blue Alert, through Green, Yellow, and Orange, to Red Alert. Blue Alert shows everything is fine, while Red Alert indicates extreme and present danger. Look at the chart on pages 74–75 for detail.

You can see from the chart that some teenagers live with most areas of their lives in Blue or Green Alert, but with one or two aspects in the problem or danger areas of Yellow, Orange, or Red. Also, as teenagers pass through normal crises, it may be appropriate to "call" a Yellow, Orange, or Red Alert. By contrast, when all is well and no moderate to serious crises have arisen, an overall Blue or Green Alert is appropriate. Above all, whether an assessment is general or specific, we must act in some way for safety's sake when Yellow, Orange, and Red Alerts apply.

Blue Alert   All is well. They are excelling in life and making the most of their opportunities. They have high-level abilities to cope with challenges. They need regular, general discussion and support.

Green Alert   They are safe and managing very well. They have good capacities to cope. No deliberate action is required. We need only affirm their skills and have practical discussion of risks as necessary.

Yellow Alert   They are generally safe. They face many personal challenges, which they mostly manage. Nevertheless, mild to moderate risks exist, so they need definite support and practical guidance from us. Direct action is necessary at times. The overall demands on them may overload their existing resources.

Orange Alert   Danger exists. Serious, ongoing risks are present. Life threats are probable or imminent. Decisive intervention by others is necessary. Do it now, don't wait. They are on the brink, although not yet over it. Single issues may cause significant problems.

Red Alert   Life is threatened. Death or serious injury is imminent. Well-being is seriously compromised. System failure has occurred. The emergency is current. Urgent, direct action by others is required, even on single issues. This is usually a now or never situation.

Forethought saves lives

To keep our children safe, the best thing to do is to think ahead, anticipating trouble as much as we can and making plans that prevent it as much as possible.

Hope for the best, think of the worst, and plan both practically and realistically.

Rainbow Alert Scale

	BLUE ALERT	GREEN ALERT
Safety-risk level	All is well. Excelling in life. High-level ability to cope with challenges. Take normal opportunities for discussion and support.	Safe and managing very well. Good capacity to cope. No deliberate action required. Practical discussion of strengths and risks helpful.
Examples of specific behavior **Important:** These lists are a beginning only. They are not complete, so you will need to remain alert to other indicators.	• Very mature and personable • Copes well with challenges • Moves through struggles quickly and well • Has equilibrium, a good inner foundation, and is well centered • Mostly happy and enjoys life • Sets goals and achieves them • Has many friends and wide social network • Connects well with others • Open to support, even when under pressure • Thinks well and expresses own opinions • Accepts, respects, and values self and others • Relates very well to adults • In good physical shape and physically active • Talks easily with parents and both know clearly what each other is feeling, thinking, and doing	• Mostly enjoys life and copes • Connects well with others • Reaches out for help when needs it • Courteous, helpful, and responsive to others • Generally manages challenges and moods well • Thinks about things clearly • Has good friends and a strong social network • Feels comfortable and relates fairly well to peers and adults • Manages most things well • Has a sense of self and inner strength that may weaken at times • Responsive to limits • Learns from mistakes • Engages in healthy physical activity • Talks with parents and both know generally what each other is feeling, thinking, and doing
Action required	Keep doing what is working.	Support strengths and success. Watch for how to offer guidance and build strength in areas where more is needed. Give information about risks.

The table can be used for overall or incident-specific assessments. Orange or Red Alerts require immediate action, even if only one factor is present.

YELLOW ALERT	ORANGE ALERT	RED ALERT
Mostly safe and managing many personal challenges. Mild to moderate risks exist. Definite support and practical guidance needed. Direct action necessary at times.	Danger exists. Serious, ongoing risks present. Life threats are probable or imminent. Decisive action or intervention by others needed. Do it now, don't wait.	Life is threatened, death or serious injury imminent. Well-being seriously at risk. System failure has occurred. The emergency is now. Urgent action by others required.
• Gets on well half the time and not well the other half • Small number of close friends, limited social network, or moves in gangs • Challenged but mostly coping with school • Cuts off or acts out in minor ways when under pressure • Noticeably secretive, withdrawn, argumentative when challenged • Tendency to blackmailing or threatening behavior • Discourteous, uncaring, or disrespectful at times • Teases others or is teased unpleasantly • Repeats mistakes a lot • Internet activity beginning to take over spare time • Finds few adults easy to relate to • Poor sleep/eating at times • Talks with parents, but with difficulty at times, often unclear what each other is feeling, thinking, and doing	• Unhappy and struggling to cope • No or few close friends • Isolated and withdrawn or aggressive and rejecting • Thinks/talks about suicide: making plans, getting the means, and arranging things • Regular depression or strong outbursts of feeling • A bully or bullied at school • Experimenting with drugs • Lower school grades than before, not learning • Drinking alcohol regularly • Joy riding in cars, other risk-taking behavior • Missing school regularly • Eating/sleeping poorly • Running away from home for short periods • Unaware of other people's feelings and needs • Addicted to Internet • Difficulty in relating to most adults • Poor personal hygiene • Rarely talks with parents and they don't know what each other is feeling, thinking, and doing	• Makes suicide attempt • Has car accident (physical injury, much car damage) • An overdose or regular drug use • Drinks heavily to unconsciousness • Pregnancy (boy or girl) • Extreme withdrawal • Incapacitating depression • In bed most of day and night • Agitated and awake for days on end • Assaults someone • Is assaulted by someone • Truants • Breaks important school rules • Serious law breaking • Has panic/anxiety attacks • Psychotic episode • Bullies someone or badly bullied • Sexually or physically abused • Anorexic, bulimic, or malnourished • Runs away from home • Communication with parents broken down
Support success and expand it. Investigate and identify problems, find solutions, help produce them. Highlight dangers mildly or strongly as necessary.	Time to intervene proactively. Interrupt what they are doing. Act now. Don't step back. Follow through, strongly if necessary. Build effective protection for them.	Urgent action required to preserve life and property. May take extreme measures. Get skilled help now. Taking over may be necessary. It could be now or never.

CHAPTER 13

Making it easy

After reading to this point, you may have the impression from us that the teenage years are always very tough. We have certainly emphasized some of the tougher aspects of what teenagers need from us. Others have described this time as a roller coaster ride, a period of turbulence and turmoil, a time filled with conflict and contention, so we are not alone in this emphasis. However, these aspects are only part of the picture of life with teenagers, and often only a small part at that.

Whatever your impression, our view is that the job that faces us as parents is usually a combination of challenge and delight. And it is also our experience that the way we all approach this seven-year journey makes a very big difference to how easy and enjoyable it will be.

We can take advantage of the many opportunities for tenderness, cooperation, sharing, celebration, mutual admiration, and fun. With some teenagers, these opportunities present themselves frequently. With others, while less frequent, we can stay alert for the openings.

Aliveness, vitality, humor, joy

Teenagers are often a delight—spontaneous, curious, creative, and vitally alive. Even in the midst of their moods, they can shift gear without warning and light up the room with their laughter. Avid teenager watchers, we are continually entranced by the energy in the bubbling fun that they have with each other. This fun is something adults can join in too. And they often love us to join in, provided we know when to pull back and leave them to their friends or themselves. Our experience is also that, by looking for things in them to delight us, we find many—easily. And by looking, we also set the tone for them, so that they are more inclined to enjoy life than work at making it a miserable, perpetual challenge.

What we can do

Here are ten things we can do to make our job enjoyable and easy:

1   Look for where they are thriving, alive, fun-loving—and getting things right, and organize lots of times for shared enjoyment with them. It is all too easy, at times, to get caught up in correcting their mistakes and not liking how they are acting.

2   Move in and engage them quickly when they show the first signs of regression, rather than waiting. The longer we wait, the more needy they become and the more they are likely to be difficult to manage (see Chapters 3 to 6).

3   Express your affection regularly and compliment them at least three times a day. How big or little the issues are is unimportant. The important thing is to keep doing it.

4   Prepare for the major changes in your life. Think of the arrival of a teenager as akin to the arrival of a new baby. Life is going to be different. Ask "How do we need to prepare for this?" "Do we need to go to 'third birth' education classes, for example?" "What activities will we need temporarily to forego or do differently?" "Will our teenagers need separate bedrooms?"

5   Organize support from other parents. This might include neighbors, friends, family members, teachers, or members of the parents group at school. Having people we can call on to come and help us is essential. Increasing numbers of parents are organizing this kind of thing amongst themselves these days.

6   Choose some areas of conflict with your teenagers. Why wait? Take the initiative by asking or demanding that they do certain things or behave properly, even though you know that doing so may stimulate problems at times. Remember that they need struggle for its own sake, particularly at fourteen and sixteen, so this has great value. It also gives us a sense of power and demonstrates to our teenagers that we are in charge—of ourselves at least!

7   Give them plenty of chores. They learn many things about how to cope with life from chores. At the same time, they contribute to the household, taking a lot of weight off our shoulders in the process. Chores also provide all sorts of opportunities for struggle at those times when they need it. Very helpfully, these opportunities are safe too. By contrast, the opportunities that teenagers choose, if left to decide for themselves what to make a fuss about, may be much less safe. Finally, chores create a wonderful opening for sharing and fun.

8   Act quickly, rather than waiting, when they need support, help, or correction. Teenagers will keep exaggerating or escalating their behavior until we do something. It is much easier, therefore, to deal with clothes on the floor instead of in the laundry basket, than skipping school, joy riding in cars, or worse. Also, the faster we act, the less momentum they develop in what they are doing.

9   Meet their needs and everything will be much easier. Fulfilled young people are much happier, as well as more balanced, secure, aware of others, and available for fun. By contrast, if their needs are not met, the problems that arise from this build incrementally. The build-up only stops when their needs are finally met. The point is that their needs do not go away simply because we do not meet them. Unmet needs are like festering sores that get worse and worse until they are dealt with—sores that will poison the whole system if they are not fixed fairly quickly.

10   Look to the future for the biggest rewards. Raising teenagers is a seven-year project. As mentioned in Chapter 11, many do thank us eventually, although they usually wait until they are in their twenties to do it. In the meantime, many smaller pleasures are available, as you will see in the "Celebrating" section of each of the developmental chapters in Section III.

Getting on with it

Deliberately deciding to get on with the job can make the process easier still. We are involved in a long-term project. To complete it, we need to be prepared to hold ourselves on course for as long as it takes, sometimes with little encouragement from anyone else.

> Pilar and Luis discovered the power of this decision to get on with it with their two teenagers after a workshop with us. "We often used to feel very overloaded and resentful. There always seemed to be one more thing the kids wanted or needed. And at times all we wanted was a quiet life and freedom to get on with our jobs. You said to us, 'What about giving up your inner fight over their making demands on you. You could decide to accept that it is your job and that you are simply going to get on with it with good grace.' Until then, we hadn't realized that we had been struggling with ourselves like that. We love our kids and never thought that we would not want them around. Anyway, we did decide, and the difference was amazing. We just got on with it after that. It was such a relief."

Making this decision has been the turning point for many parents. Instead of resenting having to do it, they just got on with the job.

Put another way, the decision goes something like this: "*I love you. I accept you into my life as you are. I know it's my job to do things for you, both things that you like and things that you don't, and I'll do whatever is necessary to help you to grow up and have a wonderful life.*"

The parent pledge

★ *I accept my teenagers are in my life and let go of any regrets about that.*

★ *I have a parenting job to do.*

★ *It is up to me.*

★ *I will do whatever is necessary to help them grow up well.*

The six
stages

The material presented in this section is fundamental to understanding teenagers, to having as much fun with them as we can, and to helping them get through to adulthood in good shape. It outlines how significantly and, at times, dramatically they change and how important it is for us to match what we do with their changes so that we provide what they need. It gives general information on the significance of the stages and how to use that information sensitively so that we take into account the individual differences between teenagers. Most of the section is devoted to a chapter on each of the six stages, with the first starting at thirteen and the last ending at twenty-one.

CHAPTER **14**

"Oh, it's just a stage"

We identify six different teenage stages. Unknown to many people, they become very obvious once they are pointed out.

Each stage has distinctive features that usually make identification easy. And they run in a predictable sequence.

The six teenage stages

★ The baby—thirteen-year-olds

★ The dissenter—fourteen-year-olds

★ The fledgling—fifteen-year-olds

★ The sweet and sour—sixteen-year-olds

★ The romantic—seventeen-year-olds

★ The world leader—eighteen- to twenty-one-year-olds.

Variability in the stages   We have presented each stage in "pure form." Most people find it easier to have the information on each stage without the distraction of the many possible variations. However, lots of teenagers do not fit the pure pictures completely. The reason is that many teenagers are living through more than one stage at a time.

As we have mentioned already, teenagers whose needs are not met carry those needs and their associated behavior forward into older ages, so their behavior in any stage may be a mixture. What they do may come from an earlier or current stage. For example:

★ A resistive, argumentative fourteen-year-old may suddenly revert to the distraught dependency of a "young" thirteen-year-old.

★ A teenager may continue to throw tantrums that are consistent with a fourteen-year-old well into the middle and late teenage years.

When teenagers seem to be living in more than one stage at a time, they are partly caught back in the past.

Usual progress   Teenagers generally go through the stages at their own pace, so there is lots of variation. Even so, the stages align with the different ages with surprising consistency. Nevertheless, young people do get out of alignment with normal patterns. Interestingly, when they do, it is much more usual for them to get behind in their progress than to get ahead of the usual age markers. Some parents worry when this occurs. However, full growth is still assured with the right help.

By way of contrast, some parents have tried to convince us that their children were ahead of the pack: "My child is already acting like a fifteen-year-old when he/she is only thirteen." However, our distinct impression is that IQ and other talents have little to do with a young person's progress through these stages.

Tailoring action to your teenager's needs

The best way of responding to both the usual patterns and the variations is to deal with each of our children as they are. We need to respond to what our teenagers are actually doing, thinking, and feeling. The information about a particular stage may help us to do this, but if it does not help, then we need to look at the information about earlier stages, or perhaps elsewhere, for guidance.

How information on the stages helps

★   *Teenagers have needs that are unique to each stage.*

★   *Each stage requires a different set of responses from us, if we are to meet those unique needs.*

★   *We cannot respond effectively to the core needs of one stage by acting in ways that meet the core needs of another stage.*

★   *We need to shift gears in each stage.*

CHAPTER 15

The baby

(thirteen-year-olds)

Colleen had emotionally distanced herself from her parents for a few years. She was much less physically affectionate and seemed intent on maintaining an impression of grown-up detachment from them. Then shortly before her thirteenth birthday she changed. She started to cuddle up to both of them and would become enamored with soft toys and animal stories. At the same time, particularly with her friends, she was still "cool and coping." All the same, even with them, she was sensitive and inclined to upsets.

Through most of his childhood, Andrew was somewhat bossy and tended to get angry when he was feeling unhappy. To his parents, the reasons for his anger always seemed fairly obvious. At about thirteen, though, he started to get angry for no apparent reason. "Just leave me alone!" he would shout with a kind of "hot desperation" in response to "almost nothing." Very soon, almost anything would set him off. His parents gradually realized that this anger was different. It seemed mixed with vulnerable distress and like a call for help. When they nurtured him he responded well.

Mary described her daughter like this: "When Dominique was thirteen, I decided that I was going to stop work earlier so I could take her home from school. If I wasn't there, she'd get incredibly upset. For a while I needed to talk her through everything too. At the shower, I'd say, 'Have a shower.' In her room afterwards, I'd say, 'Now get dressed.' I had to keep coming back to check how she was doing, or she'd stop. I needed to do the same thing with her homework and chores. Her father often helped as well. We really wondered how long we could keep it up; it seemed that it was likely to go on for a long time. You can imagine how relieved we were when this intensity disappeared in just a few weeks."

Thirteen-year-olds in brief

Each stage has a fairly well defined "start" and "end," and how we handle the central issue usually determines how things go.

The start   The "baby" stage begins when teenagers move through "the switch" and begin to feel childlike again. The level of this, and how much they show to others, varies greatly. Some manage very capably, some are liable to passionate outbursts, and others are dependent or baby-like. They may make these shifts gradually or overnight.

Central issue   Thirteen-year-olds experience increased childlike neediness. Much of how they act is internally prompted by this neediness. They can feel mildly or significantly less able to cope because of it. The ones whose childlike needs are only mild are usually excited about their expanding lives at home, at school, and elsewhere. They rise to the new challenges fairly easily. Their passions or dependency only show from time to time and are short-lived. By contrast, those prone to "angry" outbursts or to distinctively baby-like behavior may spend long periods feeling very upset and needy. The first group needs us to contain them firmly and lovingly as we would distraught babies, while the second needs us to nurture them patiently until they settle.

Normal progress   The stage progresses normally provided we respond with whatever level of support, guidance, containment, and nurturing they need. As we persist, they generally grow in confidence and maturity. If they don't get what they need, their dependency is likely to increase and they may withdraw or become increasingly erratic, irritable, or upset.

The end   During this stage, teenagers respond well to adults taking over with clear, controlling direction. Whatever the teenagers' external responses are, they are internally open to our taking over because they need it. By contrast, we know the stage is coming to an end as they become increasingly less cooperative, more irritable, demanding, and closed to us.

Celebrating our thirteen-year-olds

Thirteen-year-olds are usually "nice people" and we can have a great time with them. We will get lots of rewards by looking for opportunities to be with them and to share in their lives.

Accepting their many changes   We can celebrate the changes that occur. For example, we can enjoy the growth spurt and other changes that signal their blossoming womanhood or manhood. Our pleasure and acceptance encourage them to accept these changes as natural and can help to reduce their worries.

Enjoying their young emotions   Because they are so young emotionally, it is natural and enjoyable to sit together with them for brief or long moments of sharing. Making sure we have time to do this is important. In fact, this stage is often the last chance for this kind of intimacy, as they become increasingly detached from us from now on.

Giving loving messages   We can keep expressing our affection for them: "I love you," "You're great," "I'm glad you're my son/daughter," "You're terrific." Said lovingly while touching them, this is a source of mutual pleasure. These loving messages also help them to build self-acceptance, which can bring them rich rewards for the whole of life.

Complimenting their maturity and intelligence   We can compliment them on their maturity at every opportunity. Noticing when they do act maturely can also help to reduce our concerns about their childlike behavior. It is sometimes easy to lose sight of their talents and strengths when they act passionately or dependently. Fortunately, we will generally find lots of compliments to give them.

Having fun on social occasions   Thirteen-year-olds can have great fun with us—fun that has a particularly appealing quality at this age. So, making social occasions as emotionally easy and undemanding as possible is a good idea. Telling them what is going to happen and how to act also helps them to participate more freely and confidently, and so to enjoy themselves with us.

Inside our thirteen-year-olds

> "Rebecca, tell me exactly what happened step by step." Her father, Alex, was feeling impatient. Rebecca was crying. "Well, I got to the park, Daddy, and—sob—and I sat down on the bench for a little while—sob—and the dogs were playing—sob—and the leash was beside me—sob—and then—sob, sob—suddenly it wasn't there anymore." Alex, now even more impatient, thought, "My daughter's a drooling mess and hasn't the slightest idea what happened." This was the third leash in three weeks that had "evaporated into thin air" as far as Rebecca was concerned. Alex worried irritably, "What's happening to my previously alert, clear-thinking daughter who used to remember everything?"

Most thirteen-year-olds lose track easily from time to time. Thoughts pop into and out of their awareness seemingly without rhyme or reason. Many things that they previously understood very easily turn into unsolvable mysteries. Cause and effect no longer seem to exist. And they may go through times when they literally no longer understand, no longer remember, no longer have a sense of the previous week, day, hour, or even minute. (See Chapter 4 for more on this.) For some these changes are fairly mild, for others they are continual and long lasting.

Most are uncomfortable about these changes—some mildly and some much more so. Many feel very young or childlike and feel themselves overcome and unable to cope: "It's all too much, Mommy/Daddy." Others try to fight their way out of their discomfort, but only succeed in creating states of angry desperation inside: "Get away from me! Leave me alone!"

Very importantly, with all of them, what they are feeling is out of their control. We need to understand this. They are not doing these things deliberately, wilfully, or to disobey us. They are genuinely disturbed and uncomprehending. (See Chapters 3 to 6.) Alex's frustration showed that he had difficulty understanding this.

Thirteen-year-old upgrade

"The baby" is reworking experiences from conception to about eighteen months of age (see Chapter 7). Our job is to meet the young needs that re-emerge from these times. As part of this, we need to help them manage themselves in a world that at times seems big, demanding, incomprehensible, and hurtful. At other times, we need to help them celebrate finding the world wonderful, loving, joyous, and exciting.

Feelings   Most young people at thirteen are incapable of pretending. What is inside them is what we get. When all is going well, they feel happy. At the same time, they are easily upset by intrusive or uncomfortable stimulation. Like babies, they calm quickly once the causes of their upsets have gone. If left to cope alone, they can become overloaded and distressed very quickly, and need us to "pick them up," organize, protect, and love them. It is similar if they become aggressively desperate, like deeply distressed babies "casting about for relief." Our job is lovingly and firmly to help them to calm down, to talk about what is troubling them, and to keep on until they have settled.

Thinking   Like babies, they do not do much thinking as grown-ups know it. They do have keen awareness, though this is not organized. They focus almost entirely in the present and have little or no sense of time. Their memories go, too. While they can often remember aspects of repeated experiences, they may forget specific things that have just occurred. Added to this, they have very short attention spans and are easily distracted by immediate stimulation.

Action   They can feel physically out of control, ungainly, and awkward at this time. Added to this, many often want to lie down, sleep, or stay inactive for long periods in bed, in front of the TV, or elsewhere. The thirteen-year-olds who feel very young may experience this as a palpable force that drags them into lying down. Also, the bodies of those who become very regressed can partially "forget" how to sit or stand or walk. This makes actually walking around a big problem for them because they feel very weak and very ungainly. Fortunately these experiences pass fairly quickly.

What they're like for others

When they breeze through this stage, they progress easily and consolidate what they have learned during the previous years. Most parents would love their children to grow up easily like this. However, many thirteen-year-olds do not have an easy time and this is often baffling, even very disturbing, to us.

Surprisingly challenging The differences between well-balanced twelve-year-olds and volatile or dependent thirteen-year-olds are marked. Many parents worry about what is happening. Their teenagers seem so different, so antagonistic or vulnerable or upset at times and, even more worrying, some seem psychologically troubled. Once parents know what is occurring and what they can do, however, they usually feel very relieved. Clearly, what does not work is to become punitive, or to imagine something is wrong and get professional help when it is not needed.

Moody The swings between dependency and competence are often unpredictable. We can get caught in two ways. The caring and encouraging stance we took a few moments before is unexpectedly rejected with an angry comment like, "You never think I can do anything." Then sometimes, assuming all is well, we keep our distance, only to discover them sobbing inconsolably on their beds. They are upset about something, and upset that we don't care. Fortunately, they generally settle down quickly once we have realized that they need us and we have spent some time soothing them.

Many are also very sensitive to actual or assumed criticism. This can take us by surprise and require us to choose our words carefully.

> During an English lesson, as Eric's exercise book was handed to him, the teacher commented innocently on the way Eric had written his name. Eric reacted as if severely criticized. Feeling rejected, he blurted out to the teacher, "Don't you love me any more?" which was more the cry of a distressed child than a mature question. The whole class responded with taunting hilarity, adding deep embarrassment to his initial upset.

Very different physically   As they go through their physical changes, we may need to make major adjustments. Their hormones cause them to smell different, their budding sexuality becomes obvious, and their long bones grow. The "pure youthfulness" of the child is often replaced with "blemished" complexions, and very different stature, ways of feeling, and types of energy. Both they and we need to adjust. Part of this may involve our having to deal with our regrets about the passing of their childhood.

Also at this age, many young people approach or pass their parents' height. All sorts of reactions are stimulated by this:

★ How do we manage someone who is as big as we are?

★ Do they still need anything from us?

★ How can we cope with all these changes?

★ If they get angry, are we safe?

All are important questions.

What thirteen-year-olds need

"The baby" is standing right at the threshold of the adult world. While not yet ready to go over it, teenagers at this stage are gathering strength and resources for that coming transition. Our job is to help them to do this and to make the experience as pleasant as we can.

Encouragement of their maturity   Thirteen-year-olds flourish when we encourage their maturity, their strengths, and any signs of expanding capacities. Saying things like, "Well done" or "That was good" or "I like it when you think clearly" usually works well.

We can also encourage them to claim their maturity by getting them to think for themselves as fully as they can. Helpful questions include:

★ "What do you think the answer is?"

★ "What could you do about that?"

★ "How long do you think that will take?"

Sometimes they respond well to this kind of questioning; at other times they may seem genuinely incapable of any thought. As part of encouraging them to think, we may need to restrain ourselves from giving them our answers, for a while at least.

Thirteen-year-olds need us to support them as fully as they need, but not to overdo our support so that we block their regrowth.

Acceptance   Acceptance is fundamental. When we lace acceptance of our teenagers liberally with patience, love, and a joyous celebration of having them in our lives, they imbibe a heady brew from us. In fact, they have a deep need for all of these, just as babies do.

By loving our teenagers, and accepting them completely, we help them to learn to accept themselves lovingly and completely too.

Their self-love and self-acceptance are most important. Combined, they provide a powerful base from which to face future challenges. They also lay a strong foundation for deep intimacy with others. Accepting young people fully at this age has the further benefit of healing many old hurts and emotional injuries from their baby years.

Lots of nurturing   When thirteen-year-olds are well nurtured, they thrive. Even the ones that cope well will do better. All must get nurturing to move through this stage completely. Most importantly, provided we nurture them as fully and tenderly as they need, they will grow through this stage.

They are in big bodies, so it is easy to miss their needs; however, their needs are real. Yes, they are big now; yes, they can cope with lots of things; yes, they do act aggressively or like babies at times; no, they are not going crazy when they do, nor are we; no, we and they won't get stuck with unhealthy dependency; no, they cannot help themselves; and yes, they do need us.

Nurturing things to do

★ Feed them (make it a game).

★ Have lots of front-on and side-on hugs, and neck and shoulder rubs; hold hands a lot, too.

★ Lean against them when standing together.

★ Tell them that you love them.

★ Talk affectionately and gently to them—often.

★ Forgo criticism.

★ Stroke their heads as they lie in bed or on the couch.

★ Offer simple help and practical advice when they are upset.

When they are feeling good, our nurturing actively builds inner strength. When they are feeling unhappy, overwrought, frightened, or angry, it helps to soothe them. It also impresses on them that we want them and that they matter to us. Very importantly, this approach teaches them that talking to others in times of trouble is worthwhile. Learning this may save much heartache when they are older and in need of help.

Cost of withholding nurture and support

★ Thirteen-year-old development is held up and they enter the next stage underprepared.

★ If they miss out on a lot, they can become increasingly withdrawn, anxious, depressed, erratic, argumentative, desperate, or chaotic, and function poorly.

★ If they are very needy, they may develop severe psychological problems, such as panic or anxiety attacks, severe depression, very aggressive acting out, or suicidal feelings and thoughts.

The moment they begin to get what they need from us, they generally start to calm down, to become increasingly more manageable, and to cope with life more easily and well.

Lots of organizing   Without backup, because of their short attention spans, many thirteen-year-olds simply forget to do what they are supposed to do. The solution is for us to keep track of what they are supposed to do and to ensure that they do what is necessary.

While doing specific things, we can guide them step by step by giving one instruction, and then, when they have finished, giving the next. For example:

★ When helping in the kitchen: "Here, wash the cup for me, please." After that, "Will you peel the potatoes?" After that, "I'd like you to wipe the bench now, please." And so on.

★ When arriving home from school: "You had a good day." Talk for a while and then say, "It's time to get out of your school things now. You go upstairs and make a start. I'll be up in a minute." Then go upstairs yourself after a few minutes to check and to give the next instruction.

We need to become their minders and reminders.

Just in case you are worried about the demands on you, in our experience the young do benefit. As they grow up emotionally, they take over again. Until then, as one frustrated mother said, "Without me, if she needs to do it, she'll forget it right at that moment."

Examples of reminders

★ to get up in the morning

★ to put what they need in their backpacks before leaving

★ to give their teachers necessary papers, notices, etc.

★ to remember to eat their lunches

★ to remember to bring home school announcements

★ to give school announcements to us after school

★ to do their jobs around the house

★ to do their homework

★ to prepare clothing, etc., the night before they are needed

★ to go to bed on time.

Help with school issues   School is usually a big part of teenagers' lives; it involves all sorts of activities and responsibilities and is the scene of some of their biggest challenges. They need us to weigh in behind them and help. Plenty of discussion and avoiding direct questions help.

Notice how the parents in the following conversation make statements as a way of asking questions:

Mother/Father:	"You look like you had a good/hard/so-so day." (Choose something, depending on how they look and sound.)
Son/Daughter:	"Oh, yes."
Mother/Father:	"Nothing much happened."
Son/Daughter:	"It was all right, I guess."
Mother/Father:	"You sound pretty happy/unhappy/angry about something." (Or bring up a subject.)
Son/Daughter:	"Well, Cindy was really on to me today and I got upset with her." (This is an "I'll talk now" signal.)
Mother/Father:	"You got upset. Tell me more."

School activities needing our attention

★ checking what their homework is when they arrive home

★ ensuring they complete homework before it is needed

★ checking that they take their homework to school

★ monitoring how well they think they are doing at school and, through their teachers, how well they are actually doing

★ ensuring that they have necessary items like gym clothes before they leave in the morning

★ assisting them to make general study plans

★ helping them to devise the steps necessary to complete homework set for some time in the future

★ teaching them how to manage multiple assignments

★ helping them with study timetables for tests or exams

★ checking how they are getting on with teachers and students.

Dependable protection   Many parents do not realize how at risk thirteen-year-olds are. They need us to remain very alert to ensure their safety. Their coordination, perception, and understanding are all different.

Mita had traveled to school alone on public transport for several years. She had reliably followed sensible safety instructions for that whole time. However, a couple of weeks after turning thirteen, she was hit by a car at an intersection where she changed trains. Fortunately, she was only bruised on the face by the wing mirror catching her jaw. After arriving at the scene and checking Mita was all right, her father spoke to the driver, who explained what had happened. Mita "came out of nowhere" and walked into the side of his car. He said, "I was going with the green light and she went against the red. She didn't seem to see me." He was very shaken. Mita said, "I don't know Daddy," she hadn't called him "Daddy" for years. "I was walking to the other train and suddenly the car hit me." She didn't seem to have any idea what she had done.

Where teenagers need protection

★ *traveling to and from school and other places*

★ *handling sharp knives and hot pots while cooking*

★ *using potentially dangerous electrical or mechanical equipment*

★ *lighting or taking care of fires*

★ *using toxic chemicals like insect repellent*

★ *caring for other children (the children could be at risk)*

★ *caring for animals (both could be at risk)*

★ *engaging in smoking, drinking, sex, and drugs.*

A different type of discipline   To learn from discipline, teenagers need the capacity to think and understand what is going on, the ability to remember and to make decisions, and the skill to act on those decisions. Before thirteen, children increasingly develop all of them, but then these abilities disappear for a while. So we need to take account of their current abilities as we set consequences. Expecting too much during this stage is like punishing babies. It causes pain and distress that persist for years and may distort most of their later development.

> ## Discipline for "the baby"
>
> *We need to nurture, guide, direct, support, and encourage, rather than use discipline with consequences. This approach, along with our persistent, accepting presence and emotional availability, are what is needed now.*

To talk clearly   Perhaps because of the brain changes they are going through, many thirteen-year-olds become difficult to understand. The way they talk turns into a long, open-mouthed string of vowels, with only, it seems, the occasional consonant to give us a slight clue about what they are saying. It is another language.

We call this language "Vowelish." Listening to groups of teenagers talking "Vowelish" is oddly reminiscent of our cave-dwelling days:

"How was school today?" "O o–I" (Translation: "Oh, all right.")
"Tell me what you did." "O–in u, u I o os o–ur oo–I." (Translation:
    "Nothing much, but I've got lots of homework tonight.")
"Have you got any plans for tomorrow?" "I on oo o oo uh o–ies i oh."
    (Translation: "I want to go to the movies with Tom.")

Miraculously, they seem to understand one another, while we can be left guessing completely. We need to get them to talk more slowly and to pronounce each word carefully so that we, and others, can understand. Closing their lips occasionally really helps a lot! In the long run, this teaching is better than joining them by learning "Vowelish" ourselves. They need us to retrain them to produce their mother tongue. The process does take time, so our persistence is important. Fortunately, our efforts pay off and they become intelligible after a few years!

What parents need

The biggest thing for many parents is to adjust to the changes in their children at this age. To do this, we can try thinking of ourselves as turning back the clock to the time when our children were babies. Talking to other parents who have already gone through this stage with their children, or who are currently going through it, can also help greatly.

Modified attitudes and approaches   We build up expectations and routines by the time our children are twelve years old. When they change, they leave us with the need to change too. To do so, we have to interrupt the momentum of our old ways. We can help each other to do this by commenting when we react as we would have in previous years.

Restructured living arrangements   We also need to meet the challenges of the extra demands our thirteen-year-olds make on us. Remember that their needs are real and that the consequences of not meeting them are very significant. Most parents need somehow to find ways of spending more time with their children. For parents who work, particularly single parents, this is often a challenge, as there are financial commitments to meet, for example. Even for those who don't work, the changes challenge our established routines and altering these overnight may not be easy.

To deal with other adult reactions   This is an interesting one. What do we do if teachers, family members, other parents, or strangers disagree with our understanding of what our children need and what we should do about it? In our experience, many parents find that other adults who disagree with them try and persuade them that they are wrong.

Examples of comments from parents who disagree

★ *"So and so (an expert) says that's wrong/produces bad results."*

★ *"I've been told/read/seen on TV that . . . (followed by a long series of statements about the benefits of their suggested approach, implying that only that approach is right)."*

★ *"Would you really do that to your kids?!"*

★ *"There's no way I'd give up my job/life/interests for my kids!"*

★ *"What about me? Already I don't have enough space."*

★ *"I just don't believe that's true (with the implication that, therefore, it is not true)."*

Actually meeting the needs of our thirteen-year-olds is the important thing. So, when involved in persuasive conversations with others, try to remain open to the commonsense in what the other is saying. We may all learn something. At the same time, we think it is fundamental to hold to what each of us thinks or knows is right for our own children.

Support from others   Whether co-parents or single parents, having the support of others is a very good thing. Seeking out those with experience and understanding, in particular, is very helpful. Grandparents or other members of the extended family can sometimes help practically to meet the extra demands in various ways. In addition, banding together with parents of other thirteen-year-olds who understand the increased need for supervision can create a pool of people who provide practical support. For example, we may arrange a rotating roster of parents to pick up our thirteen-year-olds from school and take them to the home of the parent whose turn it is to care for them. This "childcare" for thirteen-year-olds can free up the other parents on their "days off."

Ten easy things parents can do

1   *Give them quick hugs, kisses, and squeezes.*

2   *Playfully pop treats into their mouths without warning.*

3   *Surprise them in their rooms with treats.*

4   *Keep track of them; find them every fifteen minutes or so.*

5   *Say: "It's time for your bath/to go to bed/to leave for school/to take your washing to the laundry/ . . . ."*

6   *Talk affectionately to them; say "I love you" often.*

7   *Sit on their beds at night for a cuddle before they go to sleep.*

8   *Make a special point of talking in gentle, nurturing ways.*

9   *Let them lie around at times.*

10   *Walk them through their chores and school tasks.*

Handy messages for thirteen-year-olds

★   *"I love you. You're great."*

★   *"Your troubles will pass."*

★   *"You will learn how to manage this."*

★   *"Come here and have a hug/cuddle."*

★   *"Talking about things helps. Come here and tell me about it."*

★   *"Settle down and take your time."*

★   *"Do one thing at a time."*

★   *"Remember what I tell you."*

★   *"Ask for help when you're upset."*

★   *"Write things down that you need to remember."*

What parents say about thirteen-year-olds

We asked many parents for their reactions to their teenagers during the different stages. Here are a few of their comments about their thirteen-year-olds.

Greatest pleasure

★ *"their excitement about being teenagers at last"*

★ *"fun, nice to be with, happy to participate in family events"*

★ *"their delight in babies"*

★ *"their receptiveness to ways of managing themselves"*

★ *"physical closeness."*

Biggest challenge

★ *"having to give one instruction at a time and having to repeat myself constantly and check that each step of each task had been completed"*

★ *"sending them off to a big high school when it seemed like they needed more support"*

★ *"the ambivalence about the fluctuations from baby to teenager and not knowing when to move in and support, and when to stand back"*

★ *"the flipping between looking cool, hair gel, erections, and teddy bears and tears."*

Most needed

★ *"good friends and family to support and talk to me"*

★ *"that decisions I made as a single parent were wise ones"*

★ *"[to understand] when to provide strong support and when to leave him to solve problems himself"*

★ *"to know more about what to expect"*

★ *"[to understand] that the regression [becoming emotionally young] was normal!"*

Big issues for thirteen-year-olds

Here is a brief summary of the important issues for thirteen-year-olds.

Expanding world

★ learning how to cope in a bigger, much more demanding world

★ having to handle greater expectations at school

★ being treated more like adults

★ learning to make decisions, to act reliably, and to understand more complex situations and events

★ learning how to have, to make, and to keep friends.

Bodily changes

★ accepting and adjusting to bodily development and growth

★ appearance of pubic and other body hair

★ breast development for girls, and penile development in boys.

Early sexual identity

★ handling curiosity about, and desire for, the other sex, shyness when alone with them and greater confidence in groups

★ dealing with individual and peer pressures over sex.

Managing vulnerability

★ keeping going when feeling vulnerable, both with familiar and new experiences.

Self-acceptance

★ forming a core sense of who they are in relation to themselves and to others by answering the questions: "Am I okay?" "Are others okay?"

★ learning to use acceptance by others constructively

★ ideally, learning to accept themselves completely, to accept their own vulnerabilities, and to love themselves and others.

Reworking baby years

★ filling up emotional gaps with love

★ needing new input to promote complete acceptance

★ getting new experiences of primal love and help in discovering "who and what I am," and current experience on the availability of others to meet their needs

★ finding out if the adult world is safe and manageable.

Early threshold to adulthood

★ starting to grapple with what they want in their lives

★ handling greater exposure to what adults and older children do and how they do it

★ managing others no longer seeing them as children and meeting expectations to act with more maturity

★ handling issues like smoking, drug use, and drinking.

CHAPTER 16

The dissenter
(fourteen-year-olds)

"No, I won't," yelled Patrick. The door slammed behind him as he stalked down the path. Christine, his mother, sat down with a thump. She was furious. And it was such a silly thing really. "Well, you're going to do it, Patrick, whatever you say," she muttered to herself.

Patrick appeared again at dinner time ready to enjoy his mother's great cooking. To his amazement, nothing was waiting for him. "Hey, Mom, where's dinner?" he called.

"There isn't any," she replied. "Your job was to prepare the vegetables tonight and as you haven't done them, there's no dinner."

"But that's your job, Mom," Patrick grumbled. "It's not a man's job, either," he said hoping against hope that this would work, but really knowing his mother was unlikely to fall for it.

"It's everyone's job, Patrick. And, as you knew, tonight it was yours. This family shares the chores—and the rewards too."

"What do you expect us to do then? Starve!?" Patrick said with angry disbelief. His mother had always taken great care to make sure that there was enough food.

"No, the rest of us are getting home-delivered pizza. You'll have to organize your own meal. And remember, you still have to do your other jobs. Miss any of those and you'll miss more things that you like."

Patrick was shocked. Pizza was his favorite food. "It's not fair," he thought furiously, but said nothing. The outcome: Patrick made sure he did his chores from then on, for a while at least.

Fourteen-year-olds in brief

As with thirteen-year-olds, there is quite a distinctive beginning and end to this stage, although the central issue is very different.

The start   "The dissenter" stage begins with angry outbursts and resistance. When in full flight, these young people may shout, provoke arguments, throw tantrums, and run away in seething rages. This is a time when the strength of bedroom doors is tested!

Central issue   Struggle is central. Some fourteen-year-olds act fairly mildly, only becoming a little more irritable, emotionally demanding, and prone to upsets than previously. Others act in very hostile ways and often wilfully make themselves unavailable and uncooperative. Whatever their style, we need to meet their strength with our own, at times matching passion with passion. As we "hold the line" with them, they learn to adapt to the world outside them and to manage their feelings as they do.

Normal progress   The worlds of fourteen-year-olds are continuing to expand and many of them take to this with delight. These young people get into struggles from time to time, although their struggles don't last long and resolution of them usually comes quickly. Many fourteen-year-olds are far from easy, however. Understandably, too, those who have lots of passion usually take longer to learn to handle themselves well than the calmer ones. Even so, as we do what they need us to do, the intensity of their flare-ups usually reduces significantly.

The end   At the end of this stage, young people are considerably more at peace. The full intensity of their "furies" has either passed, or they can manage it much more easily than they were. They become increasingly considerate of others and include them in their thinking and planning. Completing the process usually takes about nine months, if they are "on schedule." By the time they get to fifteen, they can think fairly clearly, plan well, and act appropriately, even when they feel passionate about things. In other words, they turn into delightful people. As they do, we welcome their birth into the adult world.

Celebrating our fourteen-year-olds

Fourteen-year-olds normally have loads of energy and are often driven by strong desires that are sometimes a delight and sometimes uncomfortable.

Sharing excitement   Their passion and energy are exciting, so we can usually find many opportunities to celebrate their enthusiasm and pleasure with them. In fact, we may need to remind ourselves to do this deliberately. Often a year of power plays, dissension, and discomfort can become the dominant experience for all.

Surprising them   We need to make opportunities to have fun. Taking them by surprise is one way to do this, because they agree before they work out that they could have disagreed. Ironically, some fourteen-year-olds resist having fun, even when we have suggested something they want to do too. Think of a red-faced fourteen-year-old resisting us about not doing their homework for that day, so that they can go with us to a movie they have been wanting to see for weeks!

Arranging mother–daughter and father–son times   This is a good time for mothers and daughters, and fathers and sons to get together. Whatever we do, choosing activities we will both enjoy is a good idea. Think of shopping, cooking, gardening, football, fishing, or walking. Lots of great times are possible at this age. Some wonderful moments also arise when we catch glimpses of our children's emerging womanhood or manhood. As an added bonus, shared activities outside the home often provide distractions that can enable us to bypass tensions that arise during our contact at home.

Making opportunities   Even in the midst of the dramas and confrontations, we need to watch for the quiet responses, for when they are happy, or friendly. When these occur, we need to act quickly to catch the moment. Doing something quickly is important because, like very young children, their moods can change in a flash. A quick trip to the store for ice cream, or a sudden decision to watch TV together, or to share a joke, or to go for a walk to a favorite place can do wonders.

Inside our fourteen-year-olds

"You never let me do what I want!" José was dark with anger and resentment. His mother, Isabel, repeated what she had just said, "When you've finished your homework, you can go. But not before." "It'll take much too long! I've got to go now or it's no good." As he spoke, he was struggling not to shout, a good sign. "I'm sure you'll have plenty of time. You've just told me that you've only got a few things to get finished." She could feel the emotional pressure to give in to him, just to avoid the struggle, but she was determined to see it through. "You don't know anything!" he yelled, giving up his own struggle for civility. "You never want me to go and visit my friends." "That's not true, José," Isabel said firmly and clearly, "I like you seeing your friends. But you now have to do two things before you go. You have to finish your homework and you also have to apologize to me for yelling at me. I suggest that you go and get started with your homework. When you've calmed down, you can come and apologize. And remember, the longer you keep hassling, the less likely I am to let you go." José almost pushed his mother out of the way, but checked himself just in time. Muttering, he went to get started, leaving Isabel feeling angry and distressed.

At this age, even the more settled fourteen-year-olds often feel a generalized sense of unease and irritability. They notice themselves unaccountably flaring up over small things. They also have a sense that they can't stop themselves, which is partly true, because they need our help to learn how. They also often feel driven from within to win at all costs.

When struggling angrily, they frequently feel incapable of relating to anything outside their feeling-based perceptions. Also, when they feel powerless to control external outcomes, they get even more furious. However, when the adults on the receiving end of their escalating emotions back down, they usually feel very insecure. This is not something that many would admit at the time, yet it is true. Most fourteen-year-olds experience deep relief when parents meet them strength for strength and persist with them until they do what is important.

Fourteen-year-old upgrade

"The dissenter" is reworking the two-year-old period. This is why so much of what they do seems so like the behavior of an angry toddler. Importantly, as they upgrade the experiences they had during their emotional birth at two, fourteen-year-olds make the older transition from childhood to young adulthood. (See Chapter 7 for more.)

Feelings   Fourteen-year-olds do have "good times" during which they feel happy and content. These are generally when what is happening is what they want at that time. However, many of them feel out of sorts much of the time and do not feel they have any choice about this. As a result, much of what they do is flavored with dissatisfaction. At times of intensity, their anger can become so strong that "they don't know what to do with themselves." Their bodies feel filled with passions that will "uncontrollably" explode out of them at any moment. Interestingly, they respond to these "explosions" with a combination of relief, alarm, and regret.

Thinking   Compared to thirteen-year-olds, fourteen-year-olds can think quite well, although their thinking is usually limited by their feelings and desires at each moment. They are frequently very self-absorbed. Their capacity to go after what they want with surprising single-mindedness demonstrates lots of thought and decision-making. At the same time, they tend not to include, and often actively exclude, other people's thoughts, feelings, and needs. "I'm right and you're not" is a common theme.

Action   "Dissenters" are much less receptive and biddable than the year before. Given a choice between cooperation and dissension, they usually choose dissension. They may disagree, resist, compete, shout people down, call people names, or try to "overpower" anyone "who stands in their way." All of this seems perfectly natural to them at the time and they feel fully justified in doing it. At the same time, they do not like their lack of control and seek to manage themselves as well as they can. We often see them struggling to act calmly, rationally, cooperatively, and respectfully, but with mixed success.

What they're like for others

Fourteen-year-olds have made a major internal change. They have moved from feeling very young and needy to feeling very irritable and prone to anger. As a result, their impact on us is usually quite different from the impact of thirteen-year-olds. Active guidance, soothing, and appeasement rarely work any more, whereas they used to work well with "the baby." What we now need to do is to enter the struggle with them and stand our ground. As already discussed in Chapter 7, this is necessary for them to complete the birthing process from childhood to adulthood.

Unfortunately for many of us, what works best to meet "the dissenter's" needs is very uncomfortable for us, so we resist doing it.

Struggling   Adult discomfort with struggling arises at least partly because as we struggle with teenagers they often seem to get more upset, not less. They may shout, stamp, throw tantrums, or in other ways act out with us. So it can seem as if doing this makes matters worse.

Obviously, we do not want to aggravate situations and many adults stop at this point. However, stopping is precisely the opposite of what "dissenters" need us to do. They need us to persist so that they learn ways of channeling these passions into living cooperatively, easily, and well. And they learn this through our persistence. "I know (and you don't)!" and "I want (and that's all that matters)!" become frequent visitors. When in full flight, our "dissenters" are sure that they know best and that parents and other "interfering" adults know nothing. At these times, as caretakers, we can feel both angry at what they are doing and powerless to influence them. After a while, we may start to expect and to dread the red face, the set jaw and the resentfully sullen tones. "Oh no, not again," we may groan to ourselves as we feel that anything is better than another struggle. Fortunately we can learn what to do.

Great relief can come from our taking the initiative. Instead of waiting for them to resist, we deliberately and repeatedly invite them to resist by asking them or telling them to do things. We do this knowing that it is likely to create crises. Importantly, we make sure that the crises we create are over something relatively incidental, like putting the cutlery away in the right drawer. All the same, if they need to, they are certain to create conflict over "serious issues!"

Just knowing that we can take the initiative makes it easier for many of us. While our discomfort may still arise, it is generally less and the choice we face is much clearer. The choice is between the discomfort involved in doing something that works, and the intimidation and powerlessness that we feel when we wait for them to set the agenda.

Some parenting experts offer contrary advice. They suggest that we only make a fuss over the things that really matter, like going to school, keeping safe, and other comparable issues. However, because fourteen-year-olds actually need to struggle, and will struggle anyway, this less proactive approach actively invites them to struggle over issues with potentially much more serious consequences.

Manipulative with third parties   Many of our "dissenters" are very good at "working the system" to their advantage. To get their own way, they appeal to other people to protect them from parents or other caretakers, whom they portray in a very bad light. They can paint luridly alarming pictures about how badly treated and how much at risk they are. They may go to other parents, teachers, school counselors, welfare workers, youth workers—even the courts.

In general, we think it best to get the facts from all involved, particularly the parents, and avoid getting between the parents and their children unless there is a proven risk to the teenager.

What fourteen-year-olds need

Fourteen-year-olds are crossing the threshold into the adult world. They are internally compelled to complete this transition. Still children in many respects, to become adults, they need ways to build strength of character, to expand awareness and their perspective, and to engage themselves in the adult world. When they get what they need, they settle, usually gradually, and demonstrate that they are learning. When they don't get what they need, they generally become increasingly extreme in what they do.

Extreme behavior is often an unconscious attempt to provoke us to act strongly enough with them to interrupt what they are doing and to give them the guidance and direction that they need.

Expansion of their experience
Fourteen-year-olds need the opportunity to expand socially. They need wider experience, particularly outside the family. This prepares them for even more expansion in the years that follow. Events like visits to extended family members or to friends' homes, social outings, and sporting events in company all add to their experience. Visits by friends are also useful here. At the same time, because they are inclined to act immaturely, we need to enforce clear guidelines.

If other adults are involved, we need to know them and to have assured ourselves that they will take the necessary care of all the young people going on proposed outings. Direct contact with them is important for this. Fourteen-year-olds, of course, often think they can manage alone. However, this is not a good idea. Their inexperience, poor sense of time, inability to judge traffic speeds, and the unreliability of their other safety skills put them at significant risk.

What we need to know

★ where they are going   ★ who else is going

★ how they are going   ★ who is supervising them

★ how much it will cost   ★ how they will return

★ what time they will return

While in our experience direct supervision is often still necessary at this age to secure their safety, they are old enough for more freedom. At the same time, they are not yet old enough to decide for themselves what freedoms they can handle. They still often need significant parental input. Despite this reality, they are very inclined to imagine that they can do many things safely that they cannot do, and they do not have enough experience to know this.

Three safety guidelines

★ *Safety requirements are completely non-negotiable for young people who are not thinking realistically.*

★ *Only allow freedom in areas where they have already proved their ability to manage.*

★ *Just because they want to do something and demand it forcefully does not mean that it is good for them to do it.*

Increased responsibility The older teenagers become, the more they are capable of supporting the systems that support them. For example, we can expect them to prepare or help to prepare more meals a week, vacuum-clean parts of the house and do jobs in the garden. If we have not already taught them these things, this age is certainly the time to start. Chores also give them many opportunities for the struggles they need.

Passion from adults "Dissenters" need to learn about emotional intensity, which they can only do well by expressing feelings. Accordingly, parents and other adults need to engage with feeling. This is mostly easy because fourteen-year-olds are passionate people and are good at stimulating our intensity in response to theirs. Even those who are fairly calm tend to show more passion than usual during this period. They like and dislike passionately; they agree and disagree passionately.

A simple guideline

Match your intensity with theirs. If they engage us quietly and calmly, then we engage similarly with them. If they engage us vigorously and strongly, then we meet their vigor and strength equally.

Matching passion with passion is often necessary so that our children are aware of us. Not doing so may mean that they have little or no awareness of what we want to communicate. For example, talking quietly to them when they are feeling very strongly, are shouting at us, or are internally in great turmoil will often not work. They simply will not register what we are saying. It is just too bland, too soft, too quiet, too dull. When we match them, they are much more likely to register us.

Intensity a must at times

Intensity has a place when expressing our affection, approval, or discomfort, and when getting attention or setting limits. Also, we do not have to shout. Yes, at times, a loud voice is a real asset. However, at other times, quiet intensity can do the trick just as well, or better. For example, we can say "I feel very happy (angry, confident, scared . . .) about that" quietly, but laden with what we feel at the time. Imagine someone bubbling with joy or shaking with anger who, nevertheless, talks quietly.

Conditional acceptance of behavior   "Dissenters" are ready for us to start actively teaching them how to behave properly and to set uncomfortable consequences if they do not do so. This requires a shift in what we have done for much of the previous year. While we continue to love and care about them, increasingly we begin to express our approval or disapproval of their behavior. Also, we offer rewards for doing things in the ways we expect and to impose uncomfortable consequences for things that are not acceptable.

Expectations, limits, and consequences   We have already mentioned in Chapter 9 that having a systematic set of steps to follow is very helpful through this time. We use the *discipline sequence* for this. Clarity and persistence are also very helpful. Teenagers need our clarity on what we expect them to do, what we expect them not to do, and what consequences flow from either doing or not doing what is expected. They also need us to persist in applying these consequences until they adapt to our expectations.

Far from tipping young people into "sex, drugs, and rock and roll," something many parents fear, our insistence on proper behavior helps to ensure that they are engaged with us and know that we are involved with them. As pointed out in Chapter 9, this can save lives.

Helpful guidelines on consequences Remember to concentrate *primarily on what we want*, rather than on what we do not want. To do this, we state our expectations clearly and as energetically as necessary. Then we follow up with the limits we are setting, making sure, as we do, that we give more air time and intensity to our expectations. For example, "You are to complete your homework (*expectation*)." Say some more about this and then add, "You are not to telephone Bill tonight (*limit*)."

Include a conflict in the first instruction at the times when fourteen-year-olds are dissenting actively. This approach gets rebellious teenagers (and others!) to respond to what is important, rather than ignoring it by reacting against it without thinking. For example, "*I know you won't* want to do this (*conflict*), *but* it's time for you to do your homework," or "*I know you'll disagree* with me (*conflict*), *but* your teacher has a point." Without thinking, they rebel against the first part of the statement: "Of course I want to do it," or "I don't disagree"; then they are much more open to the rest. Try it, it works!

Follow through until they comply. If they perform as expected, we give verbal or other rewards. If they do not, we apply the consequences we have already set. If we are lax, or if they manage to get around us, we end up teaching them how to avoid things. We can also easily teach them how to hold out on us until we give up.

We set the consequences so that they learn, not so they will like us. It is a bonus not a necessity for them to like us. Getting them to suggest consequences that they would find effective sometimes makes things easier. However, at this age, we may find it necessary to make these decisions ourselves much more often than when our teenagers are older.

Rules for setting consequences

1   Only set consequences that we are prepared to apply, *or we prove we are ineffective and invite more challenges.*

2   Make our consequences as similar to real life as is reasonable. *For example, expect them to face their teachers without a note from us if they don't do their homework.*

3   Apply consequences quickly. *Fourteen-year-olds tend to forget quickly and lose the association between events. So they are most likely to understand the significance of a consequence if we apply it while they still feel as they did during the incident.*

4   Ensure that consequences are uncomfortable. *Fourteen-year-olds are not supposed to like the consequences we set to discourage behavior. The options include no TV, no riding their bikes, no going to friends, or having to do extra chores.*

To reach resolution of conflicts   By resolving their conflicts with us they move forward in their development. When they or we continue unresolved, however, they can become stuck. Clearly this is important, so how do we know when we reach resolution? We know, because young people engage openly, calmly, clearly, directly, respectfully, *and* we feel mutual liking.

Claudia stopped her fourteen-year-old daughter, Melissa, at the front door. "Where are you going, Melissa? You know you're not supposed to go out tonight." "I'm going and you can't stop me!" Melissa retorted angrily. "No you're not. You stayed out late last time and I told you that you wouldn't be going out again until you agreed to come home at the times I set." Melissa moved to open the door, but Claudia stepped between it and her, and leaned against it with her back. "You aren't going out tonight and you won't go out again until you agree to what I just said." "You can't make me do that!" "Well I'm not moving from here until you agree." With that Claudia sat on the floor, still with her back against the door. It was about 7:30 pm. Melissa struggled on for hours. She tried pretending agreement, hassling, giving up, getting angry, physically pushing Claudia and many other things. Claudia persisted. Melissa finally agreed at 3:30 am!

When she finally agreed, it was clear that she had accepted what her mother was stipulating, because she used none of the previous manipulations or cover-ups. Most telling of all, she showed genuine respect for her mother and they each felt very good about the other. For several days Melissa was a model citizen. As a reward, she was allowed out and she met the specified conditions, particularly the one about returning on time. Then one day she started to struggle again in a very similar manner to the previous occasion. Recognizing this, Claudia looked at Melissa and said with one eyebrow raised, "Do you want a repeat of the other night?" "No, Mom," was the immediate response, "It's all right," and she dropped the whole thing!

Freedom through keeping to limits   As young people adapt to the expectations and limits we set, they learn how to take control of themselves. This learning enables them to succeed where just pleasing themselves does not work. Think about wanting to shout at someone and stopping, or doing the cooking or going to work when we would much rather watch TV.

We are all much freer in life when we can get ourselves to do things we do not want to do, or stop ourselves from doing what we want to do when it matters.

In our experience, this learning is often even more important for children with special talents or challenges. Over the years we have watched as parents unintentionally squandered their children's future opportunities by not insisting that they learn these things. So, if your teenager is a genius or severely challenged, we suggest that you do even more than normal to get them to learn these lessons.

Cost of not challenging fourteen-year-olds

When we do not challenge "dissenters" enough, their inner struggles remain. They have no control over this. They can only stop struggling when they meet enough external strength to release themselves on the inside. We knew a woman who still thought and acted like a willful fourteen-year-old at thirty-nine. Everything was a fight and her life was very limited as a result.

Also, not challenging them can become dangerous. "Dissenters" who do not find sufficient strength in us resort to increasingly extreme behavior in attempts to provoke it. If left unchecked, they may, for example, take drugs, drive cars while unlicensed, live on the streets, or attempt suicide. Many have died or sustained serious, permanent damage as a result. The tragedy is that all of this is completely avoidable with most of them. All they need is for someone to say "No, do this instead," to mean it, and to keep insisting that they comply. Eventually, most will.

What parents need

Many parents need support and help with the demands of this stage. We often need to stand our ground assertively, to continue to accept our children, to remain open and sensitive to them, and to meet their needs. Also, doing these things requires that we act in ways that are very uncomfortable, are alien, or are perhaps even completely unacceptable to us. Sainthood seems like it would be a useful prerequisite for parenting fourteen-year-olds!

To deal with our past   Some of us made very strong decisions when we were teenagers because of our experiences back then. Common examples include never to shout, or to hit, or to demand, or to appear insensitive to children. While some of these decisions are very important, some can cripple us. And making changes to them is not easy, even when we have compelling reasons.

"I swore I'd never shout at my kids," one distraught father said, "and now my own son won't do anything I tell him unless I do."

Yet it is important that we do change for our children's sake. Unfortunately, the more extreme the behavior that led us to make our decisions, the harder these decisions are to change. When our parents engaged in shouting matches, verbal abuse, or even physical violence while we were teenagers, they may have left us with open wounds and deep scars. However, we have more than our old wounds to deal with.

As our children reach the critical ages for us, we can find ourselves acting with them as our parents did with us. At those times, we may also feel the same feelings and impulses that our parents acted out with us. When our childhood experiences interfere with our attempts to manage our own children, we recommend getting professional help from counselors, psychologists, psychotherapists, or psychiatrists.

To get support from others   In Chapter 1 we highlighted the importance of parents getting support from others. Others who have faced similar challenges are often particularly helpful. Remember, too, that when young people get nasty, try to bully, or control those in charge, we can call in other adults, either singly or in groups, to "face them down" together. Schools do this very effectively. They use assemblies, class discussions, or send individual teenagers to the principal as ways to show what is expected of young people and why.

To make the time   Many fourteen-year-olds are high maintenance. To make the necessary time available to them, many of us need to restructure our lives for a while. Their need for time is similar to that of thirteen-year-olds, and the consequences of not getting it are as significant. Fortunately, at fourteen years of age, we can share the load somewhat because they'll often share their struggles between several adults.

Discussions with others   Discussions can help us to share information, agree on approaches and consequences, support each other, and prompt each other when we seem to have lost perspective by getting caught up in the struggles. One father was so enraged by his son's provocations that he yelled, "You're not going to have any pocket money for two years! See how you like that!" After discussion with his wife, he later changed this consequence. Fourteen-year-olds do tend to bring out "the best" in us!

Ten easy things parents can do

1   Look at them when they are asleep to see the "angel" inside them.

2   Catch them doing the right thing and reward them.

3   Physically follow them if they run away from a "discussion."

4   Give them three things a day to do that they don't like.

5   Only set consequences that you will use.

6   Make lists of the things you want them to learn; repeat these messages to them often.

7   Say "I love you and I don't like what you're doing."

8   Keep to your word, even when it's difficult.

9   Get other adults to come in and support you.

10 Make sure they do something to help others every day.

Handy messages for fourteen-year-olds

★   "Other people are important too."

★   "You don't always know what's best."

★   "You have more to learn."

★   "It's my job to look after you and to correct you when you're wrong."

★   "Think about the consequences of doing that."

★   "Use your strength gently."

★   "Cooperate as much as possible."

★   "Find out what others want and include that in your thinking."

★   "Discuss things with me normally, there's no need to shout."

★   "What you want isn't always good for you."

What parents say about fourteen-year-olds

Here are some comments from parents about their fourteen-year-olds. You will see that, although "the dissenter" stage is not always easy, there are still some pleasures to be had.

Greatest pleasure

★ *"still wanting back scratches from their father"*

★ *"their wonderful vitality and energy"*

★ *"watching them all develop"*

★ *"how much fun they could have together."*

Biggest challenge

★ *"losing sight of the delightful daughter we used to have"*

★ *"wondering if we'd ever have a friendly relationship again"*

★ *"their becoming more defiant and challenging to us"*

★ *"she was withdrawn and unhappy"*

★ *"their wanting to do things I didn't think they were ready for."*

Most needed

★ *"to know that the arguments and hassles were normal, that they needed to argue"*

★ *"knowing that smoothing over issues was not helpful"*

★ *"to listen well and be consistent and firm"*

★ *"that I needed to find personal strength inside me"*

★ *"to match their intensity with my own"*

★ *"[to know] that my frustration and exhaustion were natural"*

★ *"[to know] that it was best to 'win' the struggles"*

★ *"[knowing] that if I didn't like conflict, I should have used contraception!"*

Big issues for fourteen-year-olds

Here is a summary of the big issues for fourteen-year-olds. While many are different from those of "the baby," you will see that some are quite similar.

Harnessing feelings

★ *learning to channel and manage feelings, including strong ones, and not to stifle them*

★ *learning to think about feelings, to plan how to make situations better, and to act effectively to do that*

★ *doing lots of problem-solving with others*

★ *learning that feeling something is true does not alone make it true.*

Accepting others

★ *dealing with the unwanted demands of others*

★ *facing the need to accept that others make demands*

★ *needing to give up fighting and to learn the difference between assertiveness and struggle, and rebelliousness and autonomy*

★ *knowing that everyone has a place, and accepting this.*

Resolving conflict

★ *working out disagreements with others*

★ *learning how to do it and what resolution is*

★ *letting go of resentments*

★ *preferring respect, cooperation, peace*

★ *learning how to stand firm, to assert themselves and to use their strength appropriately to resolve things.*

Making the transition

★ shifting from childlike to more adult actions, perceptions, and understandings

★ completing the "cognitive birth"

★ harnessing struggle, usually through engaging with people in authority

★ learning to struggle creatively and to reach resolutions with others.

Adapting to authority

★ learning to adapt intelligently to authority, not simply to give in

★ accepting the value and the need to meet the requirements of authority

★ finding that adapting is possible without full agreement

★ learning inner authority over themselves.

Expanding demands

★ handling greater expectations at home (more chores), school (more assignments), and socially (more relationships, maybe part-time work)

★ facing their responsibilities in these areas.

Bodies and relationships

★ integrating continued bodily growth and development

★ adjusting to stirring sexuality and sexual interest in others

★ dealing with uncertainty and embarrassment

★ dealing with struggles with friends

★ resolving conflicts with friends.

CHAPTER 17

The fledgling
(fifteen-year-olds)

Julie was to spend the night with her friend Di. All parents had agreed. What the pair kept secret was their plan for a night out on the town together. They felt so grown up and ready for anything.

"Hey, Mom," said Julie as she let herself in later that night. "I thought you were going to stay at Di's place," her mother, Ruth, replied. "Well, I was, but then we went to the city." Her mother was astonished. "I don't believe you did that. You could have got into all sorts of strife!"

"Yes, I know, and we didn't tell you and I'm sorry about that," Julie talked quickly, glossing over the apology, but clearly with something to tell. "Anyway, we were going to the movies and we did go, but I really didn't like it much. Some boys were kind of hanging about and saying things, being really gross. So I decided to come home." "Well I'm glad you did that, but you know you wouldn't have been there in the first place if we'd known about this in advance. You do realize it's very risky, don't you?" "Yes, I realize why now. I'm sorry." This second apology was real.

"What about Di?" Ruth asked. "Where is she? Is she safe?" "Yeah, I think so. She met some friends and stayed with them. Her mom thinks it's cool for her to go out. But I don't think I'm ready yet." Ruth was surprised by this mature assessment. "Well, I'm really glad you came home. But you shouldn't have lied to me."

To the challenging look this got from Julie, she said, "Yes, I know you didn't actually say you weren't going, but not telling us when you knew our position on going to the city at your age is the same thing, isn't it?" "Yes. And I didn't tell you because I knew you'd say 'No.' I felt uncomfortable about that, too. I really am sorry."

Ruth then rang Di's mother. She expressed her concern and they agreed that future plans would only change after prior discussion.

Fifteen-year-olds in brief

This is one stage that most parents enjoy. It signals an end to the struggles, and it is a period of learning and curiosity about the world.

The start   The "fledgling" stage begins as the hostilities of the previous stage cease. It can seem like a miracle, even though we know how much effort we put into helping to produce the change. Teenagers simply transform. They become calm, open, available, and cooperative—sometimes quickly, sometimes gradually. Those who take longer may still flare up at times. However, even they are much less likely to let their passions run them and generally want to solve problems quickly.

Central issue   Many aspects of this stage revolve around bonding with the adult world: fifteen-year-olds are ripe for this and our job is to ensure that we and other adults are available so that they can bond with us. The time involved, and it does take time, is very rewarding. Without suitable adults to bond with, however, they usually bond with other adults or their peers. Fifteen-year-olds are also deeply committed to learning as much as they can, and it is an ideal opportunity to teach them many things about life. They are curious, capable of thinking clearly, and want to contribute.

Normal progress   Through this year, young people develop increasing social confidence and connections with the grown-up world. They begin to identify with it and want to explore it, often misjudging how capable they are, however. Later in the year, they may become preoccupied with fears and doubts. The feelings have somewhat different qualities from the worries and preoccupations of the previous two stages. Also, fledgling thinking is expanding, and they need to learn, for example, how fantasy can produce fear, the differences between fantasy and reality, and what is superstitious and what is not.

The end   As they approach sixteen years of age, many teenagers increasingly distance themselves from their parents. Also, their previously sweet availability ebbs and flows more and more. By the end, they start to resist again, this time over issues such as who is in control of them, their decisions, and their lives.

Celebrating our fifteen-year-olds

Fifteen-year-olds have a wonderful maturity and a consuming interest in life. We can enjoy this with them, reinforcing and confirming the great changes they are making as we do.

Supporting expanding maturity   We can make a point of noticing and telling them how competent and grown-up they are becoming. Also, we can enjoy doing things that show our appreciation of them. Part of this is noticing our own relief at not having to continue to struggle over "everything." During this very curious stage, we can share the joys of discovery and of feeding our children's curiosity.

Creating welcoming rituals   Simple welcoming rituals help these young people to bond with the adult world. They are very important and are often a great joy for all. (See Chapter 8.) We might, for example, give them a key to the front door, or expanded duties, or special jobs that are more adult. We give these as grown-up responsibilities that significantly contribute to family or school life. Great pleasure is also natural as we look to their unfolding futures, now much clearer in the wonder of their expanding maturity.

Sharing their new learning   We can easily discuss things with them and, because they love it, we can enjoy it too. We can also enjoy the learning they bring home, often learning we never had. Most of them will enjoy teaching us, if we are open to this. By encouraging them, we can reinforce their developing ease when acting maturely with us and we can celebrate it together. Of course, they will not benefit if we overdo this and act as if they are friends or mates, rather than our children who still need lots of guidance, support, and managing.

Socializing with them   They are much more sociable, often fun to be with, and capable of enjoying themselves, both with their peers and with adults. Getting them to invite their friends home, or going out as a group, are great ways for everyone to have fun.

Joking   They are developing a sense of humor. Often they will parry humorous comments with their own, much to everyone's delight.

Inside our fifteen-year-olds

"That's great Dad," John exclaimed, "I'd love to do it!" Tom had just asked John to begin to take over managing the garden. "What's involved in it, Dad?" "Well, quite a lot. It's a year-round job. Eventually you'll have to keep track of all the regular things like mowing the lawns and weeding, and other things that occur unexpectedly like clearing debris after a storm. There will be seasonal things, too, like planting the annuals, which will involve preparing the beds, buying the seed and things like that." "It seems like a lot, Dad." "Yes, it is quite a lot, but I want it to be a joint effort. I'll help you all you need and you'll only take over everything once you can manage it." "If you help and I can discuss things with you, I think I can manage." "That's fine; I'm looking forward to sharing it with you, son. In the end, you'll be the one who is responsible of course, it will be part of your contribution to the household from now on." "That's great!" John's eyes were shining. "Also, I'll help you with the heavy jobs and the ones that need two people," Tom added. "Thanks for asking me, Dad. When can I get started?" Tom reached out and squeezed John's shoulders, eyes shining, too, "Today if you like. You're really growing up and I'm proud of you."

Fifteen-year-olds are excited by life and want involvement and responsibilities. They also want to spend time with us. No longer as self-absorbed, they think spontaneously of others and take initiative to help when they know they can. They feel a naturalness and pleasure in doing these things. They are much more at ease than previously, and this is accompanied by a growing sense of self-possession and confidence that they enjoy and want to expand.

"Fledglings" love thinking and discussion, and start to explore the delights and power of fantasy. Their time sense has generally returned, along with more sustained memory, and they do lots of wondering about the future. At the same time, they often worry about things like their bodies, feeling strange, their attractiveness to others, and doing things well enough.

Fifteen-year-old upgrade

"Fledglings" are reworking what they went through at three and four years of age. Three-year-olds bond with their families, provided they are available to them. Fifteen-year-olds are similarly "newborn," this time in the adult world, and they are hungry to bond with the wider community. (See Chapter 8 for more on this bonding process.)

Feelings   Fifteen-year-olds often feel "good" about themselves, secure and relatively confident, at least until later in the year. This is when they start recycling four-year-old issues and can build up and worry over quite complex, fear-laden fantasies about what could go wrong. For example, "Oh, I'll never get through this test," "What if I'm wearing the wrong thing; no one will talk to me again," or "If I make a mistake, the coach will kick me off the team forever."

Thinking   Fifteen-year-olds have the naïve openness of the three-year-old. They love thinking, are very inquisitive, and are trying to understand everything. The cause and effect connections between things intrigue them. By discussing things with them we help them to correct unhelpful thinking patterns from the past. This supports them to expand their teenage thinking skills to include abstraction. As the year progresses, they also work out superstitions and magical thinking. Some need lots of help to let go of magical beliefs about things, much like fearful four-year-olds do: "Test your feelings about things with facts about the situations."

Action   Like three- and four-year-olds, "fledglings" are open and available, and keen to please and to help. They love having meaningful jobs. They flourish on shared activities that make an obvious difference. When feeling confident, they can act very adventurously. When feeling frightened, they can inhibit—even incapacitate— themselves by worrying about unlikely outcomes. Our intervention can help them to learn to act effectively when they feel like this, by encouraging them to think about the practicalities involved in what they face. Then, when planning what to do, we get them to think about what they want, rather than what they do not want.

What they're like for others

"Fledglings" are lovely young people, a delightful relief when we compare them with "dissenters." From tending to feel irritated, frustrated, intimidated, or unhappy about them and what they do, many adults often feel friendly, open, available, loving, joyous, and gratified. We want to spend time with them and enjoy their desire to spend time with us. However, some adults need to adjust to the changes. It pays to stay alert for any tendency to respond as we did during the previous struggles. Once they change, we no longer need to act as we were. Reasoned discussions need to replace power struggles. We have already considered many aspects of this stage in Chapter 8 and suggest that you read it, if you have not already done so.

Eager to bond   Lots of adults have a natural desire to spend time with fifteen-year-olds. These "newborn adults" are primed to bond with us and many adults respond to their compelling need. Our urge for contact with them is often very strong and we can find great pleasure in them.

Teaching, guiding, managing, encouraging, prompting, loving, supporting – in short, being a mentor – is very rewarding.

Critical   Peer groups often suggest preferences and ways of living and acting that are different from what parents want. Given the competitiveness common to young people in this stage, they also often imply at the time that there is something wrong with the adult world. This is frequently not comfortable, particularly when the comments are directed at us personally. Managing these pressures from both our young and their peers can become a major task. What challenges us is how to stay open to teenagers when they are criticizing and to realize that this is a natural part of how they work out where they stand in relation to the world about which they are learning.

Seeking sex role training   Through the years, our children learn a lot about living as women and men. This learning is usually imbibed in the midst of day-to-day events, rather than from specific lessons. From watching and listening and rubbing along together with us, they start to understand how we think women and men relate to each other, and what is acceptable for each to do with the other.

"The fledgling" is ready for lots of direct input about living as a woman (alone and with other women), as a man (alone and with other men), as a woman with a man, or as a man with a woman.

Mothers and fathers, and other significant men and women, may find themselves called on by the young to teach these things. Direct discussions are often very effective and uniquely satisfying. We can have the wonderful sense of passing something on to the next generation that only we can—woman to woman, or man to man.

Expanding their lives   Their expanding lives have an impact on us. Many want to spend time with friends, sometimes at home, sometimes away from home. Adults are often involved in transporting them to where they want to go. They are still young and naïve emotionally, and inexperienced in the ways of the world, so we need to continue to monitor what they propose. We need to ensure that the activities are safe and good for them. This often means making contact with parents and other adults to check directly.

It is worth remembering that young people of this age are sometimes very "creative" in how they describe who knows what and who is taking responsibility for what. We can easily find that the other adults have no idea that, for example, they were taking "everyone to the movies," or having "everyone to stay overnight"! Clearly, the only complete safeguard against this is for all the adults involved to check directly with each other. Make no assumptions; get the facts!

What fifteen-year-olds need

Now that "fledglings" are in the adult world, they are ripe to begin their preparation for living with grown-ups in the years to come. Our job is to present them with adult ways of doing things, adult values, adult perceptions, adult expectations, adult lifestyles. To help them to commit to these, we need to arrange meaningful direct exposure. Partly we can do this by emphasizing grown-up approaches that work in dealing with the issues, people, situations, and events that they are facing day by day in their own lives. Partly we do it by organizing exposure and contact with others in the community.

To learn about our adult world We can visit other families, involve our young in sporting activities organized by other adults, or take "the men on a fishing trip" or "the women to the movies." Choose activities that you think will induct your "fledgling" into the world in ways that encourage him or her to become the kind of man or woman you would prefer. This is also a good age for them to start part-time work. The point is for them to get exposure to the world beyond the family, while we keep a watchful eye on them.

To help them to manage their expanded contact with grown-ups, we need to train them actively. Very specific discussions are often the best way of doing this. We tell them in detail things to say and do in actual situations as they come up. For example, how to:

★ say "Hello" to someone in a group of people

★ talk about inconsequential things

★ "escape" from an uncomfortable conversation

★ leave a party or event at the right time

★ say "No" to people making uncomfortable offers or demands

★ decide when to say "Yes" to offers or requests.

This kind of specific education is ideal for helping them to develop social confidence and competence, two qualities that are flowering at this stage.

If we are unsure, we can think about what we do in similar situations, and say, "Well, what I do is . . ."

To manage peer group pressure   Fifteen-year-olds need us to monitor who their peers are and who in the adult world they are using as models. Remember that an emotional layer in fifteen-year-olds is about three to four years of age. This makes them very vulnerable and naïve in many ways. (See Chapters 4 and 8 for more on this.)

They may become very sensitive to their friends' opinions about "everything." Although approaching adulthood, many of them are more vulnerable in some ways than when they were much younger. Making things even more stressful for them, many of them are prone to getting embarrassed by us. Also, at this age, even fairly mild experiences can leave them feeling very wounded or insecure. This potent mix of forces inclines them to filter all our actions and expectations through an assessment of how their friends are going to react.

Remaining sensitive to these likely responses is worthwhile. We do not want to embarrass or hurt them needlessly. Nevertheless, at times they may need us to interrupt what they are doing or proposing to do with their peers. Doing this as easily and calmly as possible is a good idea, although strong stands are called for at times. Also, deliberately creating embarrassment may sometimes get them to modify their plans or behavior when other things have failed. For example, threatening to talk loudly about something with them while sitting in a restaurant: "Do you want everyone here to hear me?"

Examples of things they need to work out

★ who to talk to among their friends about personal issues

★ the reliability or helpfulness of their friends' opinions

★ what the real dangers are in various situations

★ how safe it is to get into a car with an attractive looking boy or girl

★ the "real value" of adult advice and grown-up approaches.

Education about life   They need us to pass on the wisdom of our own and older generations to them. As already mentioned, they love to discuss things, so we can usually expect many opportunities to explore all sorts of subjects. In fact, we can learn a lot, too, because young people have very clear perceptions about some aspects of the world. Teachers are ideally placed to assist in this learning. At home, we can make many opportunities. We can use these times to help fifteen-year-olds develop some clear thinking and logical skills. Discussing current affairs as we watch the TV news, listen to talk radio, or discuss articles in the newspapers all help with these goals. When discussing social issues, among other things, we can:

★ ask them their views and get them thinking about the issues

★ express our views about what issues are important

★ offer opinions on the accuracy of the reporting

★ make suggestions on what we would do or like done about it.

Important general issues to discuss

★ *Just because someone says something is true, does that make it true?*

★ *When someone denies they have said or done something that they have actually said or done, what are the implications of this for that person's reliability?*

★ *Are there facts to back up the assertions these people are making?*

★ *Are facts different from opinion or feelings?*

★ *Is truth a matter of opinion? Or is truth something more fundamental?*

★ *Just because large numbers agree, does that make them right?*

★ *Does shouting make an opinion any truer than when we speak at a normal volume?*

★ *Does repeating a lie make it true?*

To hone their skills   External demands continue to increase at this age and this naturally prompts a need for them to expand their organizational skills. In relation to these, they still need us to help them to use schedules, to make study plans, to meet deadlines, and to manage other organizational matters. At the same time, they are generally managing better and are more capable of thinking ahead as they plan. This enables them to make plans involving more extended periods than they could manage previously.

They also need to learn how to organize schoolwork that requires increasingly complex assignments, multiple simultaneous tasks, and the juggling of competing deadlines and due dates. They need to learn:

★ to think ahead to the end of their projects

★ to work backwards from there to the present

★ to decide what they need to do at each stage.

As an example:

"I have to get my Social Studies assignment in by Friday. It requires that I read two reference books, ask Dad about his work, and do the writing. It will take me two nights to write, so I have to talk to Dad and do the referencing before Wednesday. Actually, I would like another night for thinking before beginning writing too much, so before Tuesday would be better. I can do the referencing today and tomorrow in the school library. Therefore, I need to ask Dad when he can talk to me. I hope he can do it when we eat tonight. I'm in the middle of two other assignments, too, so I need to juggle everything. I'll only do an hour tomorrow and use all of Wednesday and Thursday nights for this assignment. I'll still have time to do the work for the other assignments in the time that is left."

They usually need lots of training with this kind of thing and plenty of support from adults. Our checking nightly on how they are doing with their homework for that night, their longer-term assignments, and any other school-related projects that they have really helps. In fact, it is a very good idea to check their progress routinely from the time they start to bring homework home from school. We would see these recommendations as extensions to ongoing programs rather than as new initiatives during this stage.

Expansion of personal responsibilities   "Fledglings" are generally ready to start to take care of themselves more. Initially, with a lot of support from us, they can learn, for example, to make their own appointments (doctor, dentist, hair, etc.), phone calls about public transport timetabling, practical arrangements with friends' parents, and to take responsibility for obtaining healthy food for school lunches.

Strengthening their wings

"Fledglings" need us to pull back from doing things for them. Like little birds with all their feathers, they are almost ready to fly. However, they still need time to practice flapping their wings. The flapping readies them to support their full weight when they do fly alone. And the more practice they get, the more experienced they will be when they are ready to, and do, take off. So getting them to do things for themselves is very important.

Somehow we need to strike the right balance here, as in many areas of their lives. While the goal is to hand over as much responsibility as we realistically can, for their sakes, we are best only to hand over what they have demonstrated they can manage well. Practically speaking, these young people still need lots of guidance in many areas from parents, teachers, and other adults. For example, we still need to monitor, and maybe to set limits, on their behavior, social outings, and expenditure.

Money management training   They are ready for us to expand their financial responsibilities. We can arrange for them to manage buying their own clothing, for example, where previously they were mainly handling personal hygiene items. We can also specifically help them to plan saving schedules for purchases that they cannot immediately afford.

We pay the money involved in these purchases as part of their allowances. Their job is to work out the budget and keep to it, two important skills for later life.

Keera took Beth, her daughter, shopping shortly after she took over financial responsibility for her clothing and other personal items. They explored the shops, with Beth picking up various things and examining them closely. She said after a while, "Mom, have you noticed how all the prices have gone up recently?" "Yes," said Keera, "they went up the moment you started to pay for them!" They both laughed.

Our active guidance remains important for some years. They often still need help on the selection of what to buy and the decision on how much to spend. Generally, we take more control and act more assertively than a year or so later when they are more experienced.

Managing telephone calls

Getting them to make a telephone budget is a good idea at this age. We make it their job to pay the invoices when they arrive too. If their part-time work does not pay enough, or they are not working, we contribute significantly, leaving only what they can reasonably afford from their allowances and other income.

Getting them to budget for their calls and to pay the bills prepares them to manage this very important expense in their lives.

Some parents get their teenagers to keep track of each call and to pay on that basis. Others get a separate line put in, or buy cell phones with prepaid cards, which make it obvious whose costs are whose. Frequently, these arrangements lead to unexpectedly creative solutions. From the first day she was expected to contribute to paying the bill for her calls, one fifteen-year-old got all her friends to telephone her!

Support for developing sexuality
Provided young people are ready physically and emotionally, this stage is a good time for selective support for their emerging sexuality. They need the parent of the opposite sex to applaud and confirm this: "Wow, I think you look really beautiful/ handsome." At the same time, the parent of the same sex can give primary coaching in "proper behavior" for a woman or man. This coaching can arise in response to specific incidents or at times during general discussions.

A standard way of putting things that you might want to say is: "Caring (sensitive, strong, assertive, understanding . . .) men/women do/don't do . . . in this kind of situation. I would like/expect you to do . . . ."

Young people often practice with us. They may act in perfectly normal, naïvely seductive ways, or try out on us ways of acting that they think are attractive. Our tolerance and acceptance of their awkwardness and naïveté can help them through the learning.

Some parents unexpectedly find themselves feeling sexually stimulated by the maturing sexuality in their teenage children. While this is very normal, many are disconcerted by these reactions. Even if we never mention our responses, our children are aware at some level of what we are experiencing. And struggling against our experiences only conveys mixed messages about this aspect of their lives. Our best response is to practice accepting what we feel.

We definitely do not act sexually with them in any way. Doing so is completely off-limits for all adults. Acting sexually would cause them great confusion, vulnerability, and damage. We need to be very clear that their practicing on us is not meant as an invitation, no matter how it may seem. They are seeking reinforcement for their budding sexuality, not a genital sexual encounter, which is, of course, appropriately illegal.

Ways to deal with fears   Many begin to think about the future increasingly and feel fearful as they do. Interestingly, their fears often involve the responsibilities they imagine they will have to take on in adult life and how ill-equipped they feel to manage that sort of thing. What helps far more than reassurance is specific experience, so assisting them to find jobs, to arrange work experience, or to do volunteer work to broaden their exposure is a good idea. It can also help for us to discuss their future with them and find out what they are thinking and imagining will happen.

At the time they are worrying, wondering "what if . . .?" or "catastrophising," we can do something effective to help. We can get them to express their worries, doubts, and fears. Almost always they will be making up fantasies about the future that they worry about.

After they have had time to express their feelings, we do our best to engage them in creating fantasies of an optimistic, enjoyable, and fulfilling future.

Reassurance rarely works

Many people have found that the more adults try to reassure young people at this age, the more likely they are to think that we just don't understand and that there definitely is something to worry about. However, what we can often do to help is to point out what may seem very obvious to us: "Yes, life is unpredictable at times, and sometimes doesn't work out the way we want, but people learn to manage. Give yourself time to learn. We'll help."

Friends   Most want to have or to make friends and are learning about friendships: how to make friends, how to keep friends, how to have more than one friend at a time, and what to do when two friends don't like each other. Clearly, this kind of learning is common at other ages too.

What parents need

Adults have an easier time in many ways during this stage. We get rewarded for our previous efforts at "holding the line." The more successfully we have done this, the more resolved the young usually are and the less they carry on with their earlier struggles. Those who continue to "act up" at this stage almost certainly still need more of what suits fourteen-year-olds.

To make the adjustment   Often our biggest task is to shift from expecting "trouble" to responding well to the genuine changes they are making or have made. After months of challenge, this can take determination on our part, particularly if the previous stage was very "full on."

To let go of resentment Some adults (especially parents) feel hurt or betrayed at the seeming injustice of their fourteen-year-old's antics. While these feelings are both normal and understandable, unfortunately some parents get so upset that they hold grudges against their children. This is actually the opposite of what fifteen-year-olds need (and fourteen-year-olds, too, for that matter).

The best course is to let go of our resentments and bitterness. We need to find some way to put them behind us and to move on. It helps some people to remember that our "dissenters" are in the same position as babies during their births. Babies and fourteen-year-olds participate in the contractions, but those contractions are not their fault. More importantly, holding grudges will almost certainly spoil our enjoyment of their blossoming beauty and the wonderful mutuality now evident in them.

We are the adults. It is up to us to get over the past. To do this, we may need to express our feelings to each other, smile ruefully, shrug our shoulders to let go of our grudges, and then press on.

To accept their developing autonomy "Fledglings" usually want to entertain themselves with their friends without parents or brothers or sisters. Some parents regret their desires to move away and be more grown up. However, we need to let go enough for their developing independence to flourish, while keeping the family in our young people's lives. To do this, we may need to teach them that they do not have to "reject" their families in order to grow up.

Talking to our partners and to other experienced parents who have already gone through this is usually very helpful. Somehow we need to find balance, because family is still important, and these talks can help us devise ways of doing so. For example, we can arrange regular family events like Sunday lunch, special holiday activities, or Christmas dinner.

Ten easy things parents can do

1   Sit and talk; take companionable walks.

2   Answer their questions and encourage them to seek answers for themselves.

3   Have lots of contact with people outside home.

4   Give "adult" responsibilities and privileges.

5   Invite them into activities with adult family and friends.

6   Check with other parents about taking them on social outings.

7   Get them to ask friends around or to join in other activities.

8   Ensure their outings are safe and provide lots of checks.

9   Applaud their growing maturity with them.

10   Get them to supervise younger children.

Handy messages for fifteen-year-olds

★   *"I love the way you're growing up."*

★   *"You can talk on the phone for five minutes only."*

★   *"It's good to have you around."*

★   *"You're turning into a wonderful young man/woman."*

★   *"Think about what sort of person you want to be."*

★   *"Talk directly to people, don't talk about them."*

★   *"Be honest, tell the truth, follow through, act reliably."*

★   *"If your fantasies frighten you, think about things you like."*

★   *"Finish what you start."*

★   *"You make the world; find ways to contribute to it."*

What parents say about fifteen-year-olds

During this period, parents mostly find that the pleasures outweigh the challenges, which comes as a welcome relief. Here are some of their comments.

Greatest pleasure

★ *"widening interests, more friends, socially more secure, and increasing responsibility and reliability"*

★ *"wonderful outings and holidays together and lots of fun"*

★ *"their exuberance, inexhaustible versatility, ingeniousness"*

★ *"their growing independence and learning without us"*

★ *"great intellectual discussions with a lot of maturity."*

Biggest challenge

★ *"the phone ringing constantly; limiting telephone time"*

★ *"socializing so much that it was hard to get him into a consistent routine with his homework"*

★ *"deciding how much to control and what freedom to allow"*

★ *"keeping her safe"*

★ *"getting the right balance between school and social life."*

Most needed

★ *"openness to negotiation"*

★ *"good support"*

★ *"[to know] what was acceptable behavior, especially social/night life"*

★ *"[ways of] balancing our expectations with the freedom his peers got"*

★ *"to talk to other parents, despite teenage protests"*

★ *"[to know] that they were still emotionally young and needed guidance, despite seeming very grown up."*

Big issues for fifteen-year-olds

Many of the issues for "fledglings" revolve around personal identity, the capacity to think well, and engagement with the outside world. To learn well, they need our involvement and to have meaningful contact with others outside the family.

Clear thinking

★ *learning lots about thinking—what to think and how to think*

★ *understanding how thinking, feeling, doing, and meaning all go together; that thinking is fundamental to achieving long-term goals; and that how people think is important when evaluating what others say and do*

★ *working together as all as we help them manage their lives.*

Personal identity

★ *making active decisions about the kinds of people they want to be*

★ *teaching them to check the consistency of their proposed actions and thoughts with the image of the person they want to be*

★ *learning that repeated actions, self-talk, and self-thought make the person*

★ *finding out how to handle self-consciousness.*

Sexual identity

★ *getting interested in boys and girls their own age*

★ *learning about getting together in groups*

★ *sexuality still forming*

★ *very sensitive about physical appearance*

★ *often self-critical*

★ *needing protection from sexual predators, information on AIDS and birth control, and guidance on other sexual issues.*

Expanding friendships/worlds

★ expanding social circles

★ often developing special friends and enjoying long conversations with peers (on the telephone)

★ making more adult contacts

★ balancing different areas of life: home, school, social life.

Bonding with the world

★ primed for bonding through previous nine to twelve months of struggle

★ now open, available and craving the completion that comes from bonding

★ like newborn babies, bonding with whomever is there

★ needing to do this with the "acceptable and safe" adult world.

Developing values/ethics

★ important early learning about the meaning and significance of issues, how to assess importance and balance different demands

★ learning that "rules for life" have limits and "values" are better, that rules dictate, principles guide

★ replacing rights/wrongs with important/unimportant and ethical/unethical

★ learning what to do when they do not know the best thing to do.

CHAPTER 18

The sweet and sour

(sixteen-year-olds)

At sixteen, Tomas was mature for his age, which was fortunate, because he had to change schools. He lived in a rural area and the city school he needed to attend so he could study the courses in which he was interested was 100 miles away. He and his parents had discussed the options. He felt upset because he wanted to stay at home. He enjoyed his family. They respected him and he them, and they all loved their rural lifestyle. Also, he did not want to go and live "alone," without his parents, even though he knew he would get lots of support from the adults (whom he liked) where he was to live.

When he went, they all kept contact through daily telephone calls and at least weekly visits home for him or to the city for his parents. The arrangement worked well.

Irena's father, Ivan, heard her talking on the telephone to some family friends. "Yes, Mrs. Pearce, I'd be glad to help out. I like looking after Annie. Would you like me to do some housework while I'm there, like I usually do?" A pause followed. "All right, that's fine. I'll see you at seven then. Bye." Ivan's face showed extreme shock. The contrast between this behavior and the way she usually was at home was almost unbelievable to him.

Emboldened by what he had heard, he called, "Irena, will you come and help me please?" She was instantly livid, her face red, her jaw set in stone, and her eyes glassy with fury. "I haven't got time," she snarled. "You don't know what I want yet. Just come and talk for a moment," Ivan said, fighting to keep calm. "I'm not your slave. I've got my own life to lead. You don't control me anymore. Just get used it." She was irate, filled with indignation at his presumption. With that she stalked off, leaving him feeling confused and powerless.

Sixteen-year-olds in brief

This stage is another period of struggle as our teenagers begin to mature very quickly and to demand, sometimes fight for, increasing responsibility for their own lives.

The start   The "sweet and sour" stage begins with another shift. Sixteen-year-olds start to challenge again, at home particularly. Unfortunately, the previous stage doesn't continue forever. That is, while they often behave sweetly and wonderfully with other adults, parents tend to see less of this and much more moral outrage.

Central issue   Through much of the year, they struggle over taking personal responsibility for themselves. Outside home they practice their new skills and enjoy their effects on adults. By acting like responsible young citizens there, they learn important lessons. However, at home, their righteous indignation is often on a hair-trigger. They tend to experience us as interfering and, depending on their temperament, respond with various levels of outrage. They struggle with us over who is in control and who is responsible for what they do. They need to learn that these are not one and the same.

Normal progress   Our job is to engage with them repeatedly through the months that follow. We are no longer in a position to force them to do things; however, we still do have considerable influence. We need to assert and reassert our opinions, expectations and, over safety and well-being issues, limits. Our challenges are to get their attention, to have real impact, and to point out their strengths and their limitations. If they do not get what they need to keep growing, they are inclined to escalate their demands for freedom, often to the point of leaving home or provoking us to tell them to go.

The end   With our persistence, they gradually soften and come to terms with their actual capacities and responsibilities. Our part is to learn to act with more detachment. It is worth saying that this stage is frequently a very traumatic time for all concerned. It ends with them feeling relaxed about taking responsibility for themselves and giving up the fight with us for control over their actions, something they discover they had all along.

Celebrating our sixteen-year-olds

Sixteen-year-olds are often very helpful, caring, and mature, even if they hide this at home. They are striving for maturity and increasingly succeed as the year progresses.

Making the most of opportunities   They mature rapidly at this age, partly by expanding and consolidating what they have learned already. We can delight in this. When they are affectionate, sweet, and helpful at home, we can also notice and enjoy these times with them. Of course, these times also give us the opportunity to discuss calmly some of the important issues that may have arisen at more heated moments. In addition, when all is calm, much more depth, under-standing, and insight than we were imagining often emerges.

Debating with them   Discussing issues with them is often very stimulating and interesting. No longer children with little grasp of the grown-up world, these young people are frequently insightful and incisive in the ways they put their views. Their understanding of complex situations is breathtaking at times. Also, any immaturity or lack of breadth in their views need not distract us from enjoying the advances they are making and the validity in what they say.

Talking to others about them   Teachers, family friends, and others are often good sources of praise. They can tell us at this stage how wonderful they think our children are. We can share these comments with each other and feel glad that they are well liked. We can also learn about aspects of our children that are hidden from us.

Enjoying their stories   By showing interest in their activities and what they are discovering "out there" for themselves, we can find much to enjoy too. As part of this, we can celebrate their developing relationships with others. While safety and common sense remain important issues, we can support many outings, parties, or trips to shops with friends. They are frequently interested in our advice, cautiously and respectfully given of course (!), about how to handle things with others, including perhaps boyfriends or girlfriends.

Inside our sixteen-year-olds

"Stop interfering," yelled Joellie. "It's my job," her father yelled back. *"Why can't he just leave me alone?"* she thought as he kept talking. "You aren't an adult yet. I'm your father and I need to make sure that you're safe." "I don't care. You're making a big mistake in stopping me. I can do what I want." She was implacable inside, absolutely convinced of her power to do anything. "I don't even have to stay at school any more, if I don't want to, and I sure don't have to stay here." She usually felt strong when she was able to wrong-foot her father by threatening to leave. *"Good, got you again,"* she thought as she saw him blanch. But this time he surprised her. With unexpected calm he said, "That's true. You don't have to stay in school, and you don't have to live here." Then, fixing her with an intense look, he said, "And we don't have to support you either." With that he paused. "I want you to finish school and I want you to have a happy life. You're legally free to leave home or school, but I don't think that you are ready to do either. Understand this, though, if you stay, our continued financial and practical support depends on you keeping the rules we lay down for you here. If you don't, we will definitely stop supporting you." Joellie sat down suddenly. She'd never thought that her parents would actually stop paying for her, or that they would really accept her leaving home. She did want to finish school and, underneath it all, she knew she wasn't ready to live on her own. "Can we talk, Dad?" she asked.

Sixteen-year-olds often experience delight in their own mastery when others treat them as grown-ups. With this taste of freedom, they want to do what older teenagers or grown-ups are doing. If blocked, they can feel enraged and have little or no perception that they are not yet mature enough to manage the levels of freedom they crave. They keenly feel that others, especially their parents, have no right to restrict, guide, control, direct, suggest, or in other ways influence what they will or might do. A common feeling and cry is, "How dare you interfere in my life." At the same time, when doing what they want, they often feel relaxed, happy, and easy-going.

Sixteen-year-old upgrade

Sixteen-year-olds are reworking their experiences from five to seven years of age. Accordingly, they carry with them a greater sense of internal emotional presence and maturity than previously. While still emotionally immature, they have found some inner strength. They need us to help them through these young feelings and experiences.

Feelings   Whereas thinking was often to the fore in the previous year, many sixteen-year-olds seem taken over by intense feelings again. They tend to enjoy things as passionately as they may dislike them. They can feel hardly done by, as if they are missing out, and that no one else understands. At the same time, very like excited children going to school for the first time, they feel stimulated about their expanding lives. This is tempered, however, with fears about how to cope and with feeling isolated and alone in the midst of large numbers of people.

Thinking   During this stage, young people are still inclined to get bound up by limited ways of thinking, particularly when they feel intensely about something. They have an increasing interest in the outside world and are active in exploring it. They give lots of thought to who is in control, who is responsible, and how free everyone is. They think a great deal about justice and injustice, and values and ethics have an increasing relevance to their lives. As part of this learning, they can act in hidebound or rigid ways about rules. Also, their thinking can easily become entangled in triangular issues involving others, much as five- to seven-year-olds' thinking does.

Action   At this age, young people usually do things with a greater sense of independence and responsibility. They are like young children at school who practice acting grown up. Because of their sense of mastery, they can develop a naïve confidence in what they are doing and how well they are doing it. They are still inexperienced, so they do not take account of future consequences, which can easily get them into trouble. Also, many of them often disregard their families, act for themselves, and take on more than they can cope with.

What they're like for others

Sixteen-year-olds are capable of acting with great charm and a wonderful winning poise. Naturally, many adults enjoy them acting like this. Also, when they want something very much, they can apply themselves diligently to doing whatever is necessary to get it.

When they set out to appeal to and impress adults with their maturity, they usually succeed. Because our teenagers often seem intent on doing the opposite with us, however, we may enjoy other people's sixteen-year-olds much more than our own.

Very upsetting   Like some of the other more testing stages, young people in the "sweet and sour" stage can push parents and other caregivers very hard. Perhaps it is the moral indignation and the "assaulting" quality of what they do at times that is most shocking, hurtful, or provocative to many of us. Whatever it is, it is usually upsetting.

> ### What is upsetting to parents
>
> ★ *their moral outrage*
>
> ★ *their willful, righteous obstinacy*
>
> ★ *their emotional cut-off from us and others*
>
> ★ *their apparent complete lack of interest in others*
>
> ★ *their insensitivity about their impact on others.*

Sixteen-year-olds seem capable of "bringing out the worst" in many adults: "I say things to my son that I swore I'd never say to a child of mine. I have never felt so angry, so frustrated, so impotent." These are common words from parents in the thick of the action.

It is little wonder that so many sixteen-year-olds leave home, sometimes pushed out by their parents. At least, it seems, we can take some comfort in the midst of our trials that our feelings are very natural and shared by others.

We don't think sixteen-year-olds are ready to leave, no matter how much they invite us to "invite" them to go, or how much they declare that they are going.

Hurtful and unpleasant   Many sixteen-year-olds are reluctant to show good will toward their parents in front of their friends. Acting respectfully is often seen as very "uncool," even if they usually get along well with us. So they go to great lengths to show how untouched by and disdainful of us they are. We may find this kind of unpleasantness very upsetting.

> Ester used to put lots of energy into getting her parents to take her friends along on social outings. When out, she would treat her parents as if they were not there. If their presence pressed itself on Ester's attention, she would act disdainfully and talk rudely to them. If they said anything, she would make exasperated eyes at her friends, implying that her parents had just landed from Mars and didn't have the slightest idea about anything.

Intrusive and dominating   Because they are frequently intent on letting us know who is boss, they do many intrusive things. Where they know there is a limit, for example, they are likely to break it, especially, it often seems, if we are likely to be upset by their doing so. They come into a room and dominate the space, try and take over conversations, and generally put themselves first in all sorts of ways. Handling this kind of thing is challenging and important, because the way they act often has an implied "dare to disagree and you'll pay" quality to it. Of course, we need to respond so they learn that their actions have consequences.

> Grant went into his parents' bedroom while they were out, took his boots off on the bed, and ate potato chips as he watched TV. All of this was completely forbidden. "But how did they know?" you may wonder. He left everything for them to find—boots, socks, and chip crumbs all over the rumpled bedspread!

What sixteen-year-olds need

Some people think that parenting is no longer necessary at this age because sixteen-year-olds are young adults. But this is not true. They still need lots of guidance and counsel. What is also needed is a change in style from us, which is now possible because they are increasingly mature and because they respond well to our support for them to grow up.

Sixteen-year-olds need us increasingly to move away from acting as controllers to acting as friendly, loving, forthright consultants.

To take balanced responsibility   They start off this stage by prematurely claiming full personal responsibility and power. They often struggle with us because they see us as denying them these rights. And, of course, we do at times.

Paradoxically, by claiming more than they are ready for, sixteen-year-olds ready themselves to take over later. We know they are ready when they genuinely realize that they do not need to fight us, they only need to act responsibly. They demonstrate this when they get on with things without us taking the initiative.

A frequent cause of conflict is the non-performance of "duties." This is a favorite way for them to try and get us to "treat them like children," so they can object to our doing so. For example, instead of taking the initiative themselves, they often expect adults to get them up in the morning, to make sure that they do their homework, or to remember their chores. In other words, they act as if we are still responsible.

Generally, our best response is to do a combination of three things:

1   We make their responsibilities clear to them and state that we will no longer wake, prompt, push, or remind them.

2   We highlight the consequences that flow from their non-performance. For example, "Well, it's your responsibility to get up at the right time. You were late because you didn't wake yourself up. And naturally, being late, you missed your ride to school."

3   We continue to seek to influence them actively to do what is important through discussion, offering incentives, and intense persuasion. We usually do this after the event, however.

Different forms of parental "control"   For most of the time up to this point, we have had final control over our children and this was necessary. However, at this age, they are no longer controllable in the same way. We no longer have the old powers to act for their benefit without their voluntary participation or agreement. So we need to shift gears.

Instead of trying to control our sixteen-year-olds, we seek to influence them.

In the past, we might have said, for example, "You will do your homework now, or you won't watch TV for three days." Now we say, "I want you to do your homework immediately, and if you don't, then I won't transport you and your friends to football on the weekend."

> ## *A different type of "control"*
>
> Before: *When treating them as children, we tell them what they will have to do or not do as a consequence of their actions.*
>
> Now: *At this stage, we tell them what we will do or not do as a consequence of their actions.*

Fortunately, they are generally maturing rapidly, so we can usually get them involved in discussions, particularly later in the year. Looking for times when everyone is fairly calm is worthwhile. Also, as we talk things over, it often helps to keep repeating statements like, "You are in control of your life now; it is up to you," "No, I can't make you do things," "Yes, I will keep telling you what I think is important," and "What you do will influence what we and others do, so think before you act."

Talking with sixteen-year-olds

We still need to intervene with them at times. And letting go of trying to control them is different from giving up as parents. As part of intervening, we may say, "Yes, I know you think what you propose will be all right, but you don't yet know enough about this. I do know and what you are thinking about is not good for you (is unsafe, is dangerous . . .). So I want you to know that I am completely opposed to you doing it and I will do all that I can to persuade you to stop. I am very happy to talk to you about alternatives."

This is quite a speech and, when said with the same passion as they are feeling, it usually has some impact. In fact, the reality is that sixteen-year-olds usually have at least a sneaking suspicion that they are too inexperienced, so this approach strikes a natural chord with them. Deep down, they know they need advice, which often prompts them to begin to discuss possible concerns and consequences more calmly. A helpful hint in these discussions is to take the position: "I support you doing as much as you can; my concern is . . . ." This approach aligns us with them and seems to dissolve our opposition to them.

Generally, when talking with us, they will do best if we give matter-of-fact, direct, clear feedback about the realism, practicality, and safety of what they are proposing to do, or are already doing. In addition, they may need lots of input on the emotional effects of their behavior on other people, including us.

In the midst of our "debates," our young people are usually greatly reassured when we say that we want to keep in contact with them as they grow up. We are not trying to get rid of them.

Remember that power struggles at this age are not ones for us to win, unlike many of those from earlier ages. Our goal is to get the solution to come from our children's own strength.

Strong, rational responses   As mentioned, many sixteen-year-olds are capable of stimulating adults to say and do things that surprise us. We can become irrational, prejudiced, unthinking, and out of balance. However, if we allow our passions alone to dictate what we say and do, then we are likely to act in unhelpful and possibly harmful ways.

In fact, their passion indicates what they need from us. While aspiring to control "everything," they experience themselves as very out of control much of the time. And they feel deep relief when adults stand their ground and do not back away from their outraged flare-ups. The very intensity that we feel with each other at these times is healing. It helps to strengthen our connections with each other so that these survive the tests of their righteous passion.

In whatever we do, they need us to stay as rational as possible. For their sake we need to keep relating rationally to issues, problems, solutions, situations, and events throughout our exchanges.

> Once when visiting, Ken witnessed a screaming match in the kitchen between a mother and daughter. Suddenly, in mid-stream, the daughter ran up to her bedroom, leaving the mother looking pent-up and helpless in her wake. When she asked for a suggestion, Ken recommended that she chase her to her room and continue the "conversation." He also suggested that she keep on saying what was important—very loudly if necessary. When she got up there, Ken could hear the mother yelling things like "I love you; that's why I'm doing this," "I don't think what you're doing is sensible; tell me why you think it's important" and "It's your safety that matters to me; not controlling you." All of this was very sensible, as were many of the shouted replies. Within half an hour, they were both back in the kitchen feeling very good about each other.

Once calm is restored, further discussions often help to clarify and reinforce mutual concerns and to formulate sensible shared plans.

Parents becoming consultants   When things go well, the end of this year will see us mostly acting as consultants to our children. In fact, it may take the full year to achieve this result. Exchanges are often anything but consultative in the beginning. All the same, even when we have to meet strength with strength, we do so only to get and hold their attention, or to prevent them steamrolling us. Thankfully, as the year progresses, we can expect things to get easier. Our children usually become more respectful and flare up less often; and once having flared up, they calm down more quickly.

In the end, we advise and counsel, seeking their agreement. We pull back from trying to make them do what we think is best.

Further support for their sexuality   Young people at this stage are often physically mature and can seem much older than they are. However grown up they look, they are generally much less sure of themselves than they pretend and can still very easily be "bruised emotionally." They are also often very concerned about their sexual attractiveness and how intensely sexual they feel at times. They are quite capable of showing tenderness in romantic encounters and of feeling love and sexual passion. In natural attempts to learn what to do, they may develop crushes on adults like teachers or family friends with whom they feel safe.

These changes are a passionate extension of past learning. Parents and other adults need to act with sensitivity here, so that teenagers can continue to develop confidence in their sexuality. As part of this, when necessary, we need to give appropriate guidelines about how to act with us: "I love the way you are growing up, and what you have just done with me is not appropriate. That's the sort of thing to do with a boyfriend/girlfriend." Adults need to understand that the young are mimicking adult courting/sexual behavior and are practicing with us. As mentioned in the last chapter, adults need to restrict themselves completely to nonsexual exchanges with them.

Mentors   Given how well they can get along with adults at this age, it is natural that they seek out mentors. Frequently they select adults wonderfully well—people who can fill in the gaps they have, or can help to heal old wounds that still trouble them. Once teenagers find people like this, they understandably often want to spend increasing amounts of time with them. And these feelings are often mutual.

Parents can feel rather left out, even rejected, by these new relationships, particularly if their children play them off against their newfound friends. Also, some people are unsuitable, and we may need to do something if we find their selections are not good for them. However, provided we have assured ourselves that our children are in good hands, our best move is generally to step back and celebrate.

Mentors give teenagers the chance to learn important lessons from other adults who are willing to take an interest in them. Many wonderful learning opportunities arise naturally like this.

One sixteen-year-old left home "without permission" to live with her boyfriend's family. She was very attracted to their way of living. However, upon checking, her mother discovered that they were well-known criminals in the area. She then went to visit the family and refused to leave until her daughter left with her. When she wouldn't leave, her mother called the police. Although they had no legal right to remove the daughter, the police persuaded her to go with them "for a talk at the station." During that talk, the sergeant told her very clearly how much she was putting herself at risk. She was very shocked and did not go back.

Help with school or work demands   Sixteen-year-olds usually face a big increase in demands on them at school, if they are still attending, or at work, if they have left school. In addition, they are not capable of looking forward and seeing what is ahead and they often hear all sorts of stories about how hard life will be. In this context, persistence can become a big issue.

Teenagers need support from us to persist and to deal with their urges to give up their studies or work. They need to learn to face life, even if it is hard. Our support in this is essential.

More learning on thinking   Sixteen-year-olds are still learning to think clearly and flexibly. Happily, we can encourage them in this fairly easily because, even in the midst of their passions, they think a lot and love to debate issues.

They are intrigued by issues of right and wrong. They are also very interested in how to know what is real and what is not, and what values are important. Our discussions can take on a strongly philosophical quality as they practice their conceptual abilities and develop their own value systems. They are moving on from a rigid interest in rules of right and wrong to discovering principles to guide them in how to act in different situations. Other hot issues are to do with reality and who determines it. These developments show real advances and are very exciting and often stimulating.

Be prepared, however, because they usually discuss things passionately, not neutrally. Sixteen-year-olds often push the limits of adult thinking and values, and often try out new approaches in various parts of their lives as a result of their discussions.

Coaching sixteen-year-olds in their thinking

★   *"I'm impressed by the way you're thinking about this,"* then specify what it is that impresses us.

★   *"I think there is more to this,"* when they need to expand their thinking or to consider things differently.

★   *"I expect clearer thinking from someone with your intelligence,"* when they put people down, or allow their feelings to hijack their thinking processes, followed by *"I would prefer you to . . . ."*

What parents need

The parents of young people who breeze through this stage will probably wonder what the fuss is all about. Well, the fuss is about the fuss that a very large number of sixteen-year-olds do make.

Mutual support　　During this high-demand time, parents, teachers, and others usually benefit from supporting each other. We can:

★ back each other up

★ clarify our position with each other, so that in the midst of the struggles we remain as aligned as possible

★ remind each other of what was decided, should one or more of us start to waver

★ interrupt the action and have a discussion, something that usually catches a teenager's attention, if issues arise that we have not already discussed

★ debrief with someone after dealing with trying incidents.

Discussions like this enable us to blow off steam and then to make sensible plans for what to do next time if, perish the thought, there is a next time! Remember, too, that lots of others have already dealt with sixteen-year-olds, so let's talk to them for encouragement.

To persist through the change　　As mentioned, it may help to realize that the struggles are a sign that teenagers are almost ready to take the responsibility they are craving. The ends of lots of significant transitions in life are like this. *Generally, at these times, the more hopeless we feel, the closer teenagers are to finishing some important learning, and the more important it is for us to persist.* Many women experience this during childbirth. During transition, right at the point that the delivery is about to begin, is when the greatest doubts, worries, anxieties, fears, and anger—the greatest passions—often occur. Our feelings are a sign that we are almost there and we need to keep going.

Helpful retorts   Many adults feel empowered by having a collection of simple retorts to use to interrupt the power plays that teenagers run at times. And we can have lots of fun devising them. Sixteen-year-olds are often nonplussed when we come back immediately with something. So convinced are they that their realities are the only ones that they do not conceive that adults can find ways to deal with them. Try these two:

★ "You can't make me help with the dishes." We reply, "That's true and I'm not going to try. But you can't stop us putting the dirty ones in your bed, either."

★ We say, "You're late." They say, "Get used to it. I'm not a child any more!" "Really!?" (said with surprised delight).

Explaining legal rights and household duties

Parent: *"What we do for you now that you are sixteen is completely voluntary. We don't have to do this anymore. Realize this. You are here because we want you here, not because we have to look after you."*

Young person *(rolling his/her eyes and sighing)*: *"Well, I don't have to stay either!"*

Parent: *"That's true. You can get a job or go on the dole. You can leave school. There's nothing we can do to stop you legally."*

Young person *(challengingly)*: *"So what's your point?!"*

Parent: *"My point is for you to remember something, especially if you want things from us. If you act well, we will keep supporting you and you can go on living here. But if you act unpleasantly a lot of the time, we might decide to withdraw our services and support from you completely."*

Young person: *"You mean that I might have to leave?"*

Parent: *"Yes, it could get to that. But we may withdraw many of our other services to you long before then. So I suggest you think carefully and act cautiously."*

Young person: *"Hmm. All right, I'll think about it."*

Parent: *"Good, we're not joking."*

Ten easy things parents can do

1 Ask others how wonderful our sixteen-year-olds are.

2 Express our opinions to our teenagers when we disagree with them, even if they get upset.

3 Set curfews and expect them to abide by them.

4 Withdraw services as consequence for misbehavior.

5 Make the most of the sweet times by having fun.

6 Agree when they say, "It's my life."

7 Make helpful suggestions about things daily.

8 To complaints, ask: "What are you going to do about it?"

9 Say, "I want you to leave as soon as you're ready, just not yet."

10 Tell them that we want to be friends with them in the future.

Handy messages for sixteen-year-olds

★ "I'm really enjoying you growing up and I'm looking forward to you taking over your own life completely. It won't be long."

★ "You are a family member while you live here and that involves doing your jobs. Do such and such now."

★ "We react to what you do. If you want our good will, then behave properly. If you don't, we'll withdraw our support."

★ "We see for ourselves (hear from others) that you are a wonderful person. We like this."

★ "We want you to be in charge of your life. You don't need to fight us to get that. However, we won't pretend with you when you're wrong or when you aren't acting responsibly."

★ "Yes! It's your life—and it's up to you to deal with the consequences of what you do."

★ "No, we can't control you. That's your job now. But, our opinions are still worthwhile and we will keep contributing them for as long as you live here."

What parents say about sixteen-year-olds

As we have seen, sixteen-year-olds are aptly titled "sweet and sour." They amaze our friends with their delightful behavior, yet they can be rude to and disdainful of us. Here is how some other parents have described living with them.

Greatest pleasure

★ "his enthusiasm about things he liked doing (playing games on computer, rock climbing, etc.)"

★ "finding new ways to get things done"

★ "having their many friends visiting"

★ "her strong sense of justice and awareness of others' needs"

★ "signs of a fantastic young adult emerging."

Biggest challenge

★ "he was rude, with no concern for others, particularly [us]"

★ "[their] making decisions without heeding our wishes"

★ "our setting standards about parties and alcohol"

★ "their keeping relationships open with their friends and us"

★ "her defiance against any rules."

Most needed

★ "to talk with other parents during this time"

★ "a way to work out what to do (for example, being asked by another parent, 'What worked with you when you were sixteen?' and 'What didn't?')"

★ "to know it was still important to make time and be available"

★ "to know that 'this too will pass,' that holding the boundaries was still important, that he wasn't an adult yet"

★ "to know that yelling at each other was okay and necessary at times"

★ "to negotiate the setting of boundaries more than before."

Big issues for sixteen-year-olds

Two recurring themes in our exchanges with sixteen-year-olds are about taking responsibility for and assuming control of themselves. They need to learn that the way to do these things is to stop fighting and to accept that they already have them.

Taking responsibility

★ *answering the questions, "Who is responsible for me?" and "Who am I?"*

★ *learning that autonomy and rebelliousness are different, and that claiming power is different from willfulness*

★ *making the decision, "I am responsible for me and my life."*

Control

★ *accepting control of themselves*

★ *letting go of fighting others for that control*

★ *learning to negotiate openly and cooperatively over activities, chores, and consequences*

★ *acceptance of the reality that parents have power over the services they offer*

★ *acceptance that others "rightly" set conditions for making themselves and their services available*

★ *learning how to seek to influence people when not in control, people who, for example, do drugs, drive dangerously, drink too much, express disagreeable opinions.*

Parents as consultants

★ *moving toward using parents as friendly consultants*

★ *seeking guidance*

★ *accepting with good grace strong recommendations, even strict limits, enforced by the withdrawal of parental services*

★ *defining parents as allies, not contestants or "enemies."*

Fears about the future

★ realizing that they are close to taking over their lives

★ discovering how to connect with others who can help with this

★ accepting that many of life's events are not controllable

★ beginning to find ways of managing the unknown.

Maturing sexuality

★ learning to deal with sexual interest, both their own in others and others in them

★ getting guidance and modeling from adults

★ making decisions, if not made already, about how to handle sexual encounters (for example, limits and how to manage them)

★ getting used to being one of a couple if going steady.

Dealing with triangles

★ relating to more than one person at a time

★ keeping multiple friends

★ being the odd one out

★ sharing time and attention

★ acting directly without attempting to manipulate others

★ communicating directly with others, not about them through others.

CHAPTER 19

The romantic

(seventeen-year-olds)

Seventeen-year-old Jesse Martin set out alone to sail around the world from Australia via Cape Horn. His yacht's name, *Lionheart*, had clear echoes of Robin Hood and Richard the Lion Heart. Watching and listening to him on TV, he impressed as a practical, quiet young man. Although he understated it, he seemed very taken with the daring and romance of his project. While some people thought the whole idea was crazy and dangerous, his parents backed him fully. One clip of him on TV included a side shot with him in the bow of his yacht. He was looking ahead into the distance, his longish blond hair blown back by the light breeze into which he was sailing. He looked like a Viking! Wonderful stuff.

"She used to come home at seventeen and talk to me every day, sometimes for hours." Isobel was obviously reliving her pleasure at these times as she spoke. "It often didn't seem to matter what I said. She just seemed to want to talk things out with someone. At other times, though, she was very keen to find out what I thought. She would listen, too, and then go away and try any advice I offered. They were lovely times. We used to share in other ways before, but this was much more mature, more adult."

Graham was just home from a two-week school trip to Asia. It was his first time away from home for an extended period and his first time out of the country. When he got back, he was full of exuberance and talked about the trip at length. His parents told us a day later about his arrival home, saying, "Graham said, 'It was the best two weeks of my life.'" Then with a shared laugh they added, "We're trying not to take offense at this." The tension between their delight at his setting out on his own and their desire to remain important to him was very obvious. He, of course, was blissfully unaware of these subtleties!

Seventeen-year-olds in brief

The increasing desire to learn during the last two stages and the resolution of the struggles in the last one have paved the way for the emergence of a responsible and likeable young adult.

The start   The "romantic" stage begins with young people becoming much easier—sometimes quickly, sometimes more gradually. As at the beginning of the "fledgling" stage, the changes they make at this point are very welcome. Because of the intensity of the previous stage, particularly for parents, we often breathe a collective sigh of relief. Thankfully, they will now usually act very differently.

Central issue   Exercising responsibility for themselves is central. They organize themselves, make plans and follow through on them, are increasingly considerate and sensitive to others, and fulfill their household and other duties. As they do, they learn about the benefits and the consequences of taking personal responsibility. They still have lots to learn and enjoy the learning, which is something we can celebrate with them. In fact, a general feature of this stage is that they are ripe for these new challenges and generally enjoy what they need to do to learn to meet them.

Normal progress   Our job continues to include watching to ensure that they are both thinking clearly and taking account of likely hazards or disruptions to their plans. Also, they tend either to idealize or to demonize people, situations, and events, so they frequently need advice to help them to develop balanced views. Often busy with school or other work, they may have many related issues to deal with, such as study, examinations, work relationships, and handling the pressures they are under. Adult involvement needs to shift increasingly into joint ventures in which we interact with them as colleagues. If they don't get what they need to progress, they may revert to fighting us or being passive so that others act for them.

The end   The end of this stage is signaled by increasing detachment from us and increasing interest in attaching to people and groups outside the home. They become very self-possessed and autonomous. They are about to walk out into the world in a big way.

Celebrating our seventeen-year-olds

The increased autonomy of our seventeen-year-olds results in many wonderful ways of having fun. This is often a happy time, so many options open up naturally.

Sharing their excitement   We can join in their romantic adventures with them by discussing what they are passionate about. The way to do this is to share in the fantasies with them. "Oh yes, I love that too. And what about . . .?" In this way, we enter the adventures with them and set aside the desire to remind them of practicalities.

Sharing adult activities and discussions   With a little thought, we can often initiate many attractive adult activities that we can all share. Also at this age, they love discussion: current affairs, the implications of TV programs, social issues that arise from school, their friends—all sorts of things. This is often fun for adults too. All the same, they may prefer to spend their time with friends, rather than family. So it is good to have some high priority family events that everyone is "encouraged" to attend. This helps to stop them shunting the family aside completely with their intense enthusiasm for other activities.

Inviting them home with their friends   Inviting boyfriends, girlfriends, and others along to share in activities is great. As well as "drop in anytime" invitations, festive occasions like birthday parties and other celebratory days are ideal. Through them our young people learn to see their homes as places to hang out, and we get to know them with their friends. We may greatly enjoy both.

Supporting their successes and interests   A wonderful way to celebrate is to notice their successes and to join in with the praise others give them. We can also celebrate, for example, by putting on a special meal at home or going out for one. Some seventeen-year-olds have particular interests like mechanical work, arts and crafts, sports, dancing, or art. We can often attend related events as part of their support team or as non-intrusive participants. In this way, we get to celebrate with them, while honoring their desire for some obvious detachment from us in front of their peers.

Inside our seventeen-year-olds

"Mom, it really will be all right. I know it will. He's so nice and we get along so well." Gail was sitting on the couch with her mother. She was smiling serenely, completely confident in what she was proposing. Bernadette wasn't so sure. "Gail, it seems so simple to you to travel all the way to the UK to visit Carl and his family for a few weeks, but for me it isn't that simple." "But, Mom, he's going to be there and I'll be staying with his family. It's sure to be all right." "I know you think this, Gail, but you've only known this young man for a few days. He's 21 and you're 17 and, although I've spoken to his mother and she seems like a sensible person, I don't think you're experienced enough to do this alone." "Oh, Mom, you're always looking for how things can go wrong. I'll be all right."

The sequel was that she went, enjoyed herself up to a point, but spent lots of time alone at home with her boyfriend's mother with whom she didn't get on particularly well. She returned home much wiser and with greater understanding of her mother's reservations.

Seventeen-year-olds can become entranced with the idea of something, often finding it difficult to relate to situational facts. This can go in two main directions: either everything will be fine, or nothing will work out. Their hopes and feelings about what they fantasize will happen can wipe away all else: "Oh, I'm sure it'll be all right, Mom," or "Nothing is going to work out." In other words, they romanticize or "catastrophize." When romanticizing, they feel free to act on their fantasies. When catastrophizing, they may so inhibit themselves that they do nothing. Rational discussion often has little impact at the time, because their feelings hold sway. In the long run, however, they seem able to relate to what is said, particularly if they have some experience to draw on.

Their interest in ideas and values may occupy them at length. With each situation, they may wonder about the situation itself, the right thing to do, how to do what is required, other people's roles and responsibilities, and where family and friends fit with it all.

Seventeen-year-old upgrade

"Romantics" are upgrading what they went through between seven and nine years of age. While definitely and noticeably more mature, they often still carry a naïve innocence with them. They are also often uncertain of themselves, particularly when in groups.

Feelings   Just as when they were seven to nine, seventeen-year-olds can feel both more confident internally and more uncertain about where they belong in relation to others. They are generally much calmer than in the previous stage, although their passions (romantic or catastrophic) can sweep aside their rational abilities. They can feel distressed to discover that "the rules of right and wrong" no longer apply as they seemed to before. Seeking a solution, they try and work out general approaches, or values, that will transfer to other situations. Also, just as when they were young, they frequently have strong feelings about who is "in" and who is "out" of their peer group.

Thinking   At both school and at home, their thinking germinates, grows, and blossoms, drawing its nourishment from the ground of the feelings they now experience. With a greater internal sense of themselves, many seem more confident about expressing their views, although many are still vulnerable to criticism. They frequently experience issues with others in terms of what is "right" or "wrong." This echoes the ways they learnt to think about being "good" and not being "bad" when children. Their interest in discussing duties, responsibilities, obligations, rights, and freedoms help them with this. Many of them can also think and plan well in relation to familiar tasks.

Action   Their persistence with tasks and their capacity for planning and organization are obvious. The levels of these depend significantly on how well they learned before and their previous patterns. Their worlds are expanding, so they are often faced with the need to stand by their principles when others want to do things with which they disagree, for example, drug-taking, driving after drinking alcohol, sexual activity, or doing things that they know their parents have warned against.

What they're like for others

Seventeen-year-olds become increasingly self-sufficient and level-headed. Their developing prowess and capacity for problem-solving are a delight. Given the previous year, they can take us by surprise at times, too, as they move to new levels of maturity and cooperation.

> Frieda's parents had encouraged her to look for part-time work for some months and had met great resistance. Frieda had worked at a succession of jobs from when she was sixteen. Then she was offered a job in a bakery that she wanted to take. However, while enthusiastic about her taking the job, her parents advised against it, because on one day a week the start time was 5:30 a.m. She had a big study load and they were concerned about the disruption to her sleep that this would cause. Her father said, "Oh well, I'm sure you'll find something else." To encourage her, since her enthusiasm was in marked contrast to her previous resistance, he added, "You've done well to get this offer." "Oh, no," she replied immediately and unexpectedly, "I'm going back to ask if I can start later, like at 7:00 a.m." This is precisely what she did and the baker agreed. Her parents glowed with pride.

Companionable and rewarding   When things are going well, seventeen-year-olds can turn into real companions. They like hanging out with grown-ups, letting adulthood rub off on them. They are often clear thinking and very task-oriented, having turned into "responsible citizens." Also, because we no longer live with an immature young person who is fighting us to take on adult responsibilities that we are actually encouraging, we can enjoy a new freedom.

While all is not finished, the end is definitely in sight.

This is a great time for parents and others who have raised these young people. We often feel a wonderful sense of fulfillment and completion. Rewarding friendships flavored with mutuality and equality can start to flourish.

A test of adult commitment

At times, seventeen-year-olds test how committed we are to their emerging adulthood. Many of us find it easy to encourage them directly and enjoy the process of doing so. However, what is sometimes more of a challenge is dealing with them trying to pull us into supporting a dependency that they have outgrown.

> Oscar got up late to go to school. Arriving in the kitchen looking dejected, he said, "Will you take me, Mom?" "No, I haven't got time today," she replied. "But I'll be late for school," he whined. "No," she reasserted firmly, "it's your responsibility to get yourself to school on time." "But I'll be late," he repeated, turning up the dial on the complain-o-meter. "No, I can't this morning, I have other things to do that are important." "But I'll miss the bus." "No, I'm not going to; it's your responsibility to get yourself to school on time." Giving up, but angry, Oscar made for the door. Then, pitched just so she heard him, he muttered over his shoulder, "And I thought you cared about my education." His dejected back disappeared down the path as his mother watched secretly.

Maturely enjoyable

With their release from the power struggle with their parents, they relax in other areas too. Everyone benefits. They show much more mature respect for their peers and others, and often delight in this. Referring back to the way they used to think and feel with rueful smiles, they often now recognize how much easier their new ways of experiencing life are. They show a natural desire to act sociably, and to link with others warmly and deeply.

The rewards for everyone are usually immediate, and seventeen-year-olds enjoy them too. They are now more autonomous and have a natural recognition of others as separate individuals. This prompts them to take an interest in and explore what makes people tick. The sharing available in groups is also naturally attractive, and they seek contact and thrive on the pleasure of group experiences.

What seventeen-year-olds need

"The romantic" is pulling together many lessons from previous stages. They go through a wonderful period of consolidation and, with this, comes expansion into new areas of life as they test both old and new skills.

Reinforcement of their maturity

They need us to encourage their maturity. They still feel frail in many ways and our responses matter to them. When we celebrate their mature actions, they gain strength. If, however, we block them, criticize unthinkingly, or seem to pull them down, they usually feel discouraged and weakened by our actions.

They flourish on grown-up discussions on all sorts of issues, and love to ask questions and discuss thought-provoking subjects. In accord with this, responding directly and clearly, without filtering information as we once did because they were too young, is best.

We need to make a transition to giving reminders about needs and obligations, rather than continuing to take responsibility for making sure they get things done.

Balanced workloads at home

Part of reinforcing their maturity is to expect more of them. They are ready for more responsibility and by giving it to them we help them to strengthen the "responsibility muscles" they are already flexing in their lives. So, for example, we can give them more jobs to do at home, work, or school. At home, we might widen their existing duties, like getting them to take full responsibility for at least two meals a week, instead of cooking only one. Or we might give them something new to do, like keeping track of the household petty cash or paying specified bills when they arrive. Making them fully responsible in some area in which they already contribute is also useful.

The importance of balance

We all need to keep a balance. If young people have heavy work or study loads, there is a case for adapting what they do. However, the operative word is "adapting," not "removing." We think it is very important for teenagers to contribute significantly, even when they are under pressure. Pressure in itself is not sufficient reason for us to relieve them of their regular duties.

As adults, most of us do not have someone else to take over when we have a lot to do. And our job is to prepare teenagers for adult life as it actually is. All the same, under special circumstances, we can appropriately reduce the load a bit. Exam times and when there is an unusual load at work are two examples. In fact, having their other duties to perform can provide very helpful opportunities for a change of pace that will improve their performance elsewhere. When studying, for example, regular breaks help clear their systems so they can remember, think, and work more easily and productively.

Lessons on womanhood/manhood   At this age, they need us to honor and appreciate their maturing sexuality. By remaining alert, we can recognize the many different ways that they get us to teach them what they need to know. A short list of these areas includes how to:

★ be attractive as a sexually mature young woman or man

★ spend time with their partners alone or with other people

★ talk to each other about "relationship problems"

★ stay true to themselves when they love someone

★ make decisions in cooperative ways that honor all involved.

Parents of the opposite sex have the job of helping to launch young people into sexually mature adulthood. Fathers with their daughters and mothers with their sons do this by showing their pleasure in the womanhood or manhood of their children. Parents of the same sex do something similar, although their job is to show what to do by example.

Nurturing mature sexuality

Fathers and mothers need to deliberately show genuine manly or womanly appreciation of their children as young women or young men. This helps because fathers "germinate" the seed of womanhood in their daughters and mothers "germinate" the seed of manhood in their sons through their appreciation. Doing this prompts and encourages their sexual identities to grow in health and strength to full maturity.

As in previous stages, they may practice on us, too, which may still come as a surprise at times. One father was nonplussed one day when his seventeen-year-old daughter came into the room while he was sitting on the couch, walked up behind him and kissed him on the top of the head with a lover's possessiveness and sensuality.

Giving advice on how adults relate

Teenagers need active feedback and guidance from us, because they are still naïve socially. Of course, teenagers are also prone to embarrassment in this area, so we need to tread carefully. Here are some ideas:

★ *"That's lovely and it's something to save for your boy/ girlfriend."*

★ *"If you do that with other adults, they could get very confused because it's too intimate; I suggest that you . . . instead."*

★ *"That is not the way I like to see any man/woman talking to a woman/man; I would like you to do such and such."*

We can give our feedback indirectly, too, by appearing to talk about other things. For example, while watching TV, we could say: "Oh, I don't like men/women acting in that way. They look like . . . to me when they do that. And not many people like that sort of person" or "That's great! Did you see what he/she did just then?"

Consultant parents   For their benefit, we need to remember that we have become consultants, or are striving to do so. They now have responsibility for themselves, although we continue to prompt from the sidelines. Notice the style of the following discussion about homework:

> When running three days late, John says, "Dad, will you give me a note to take to school about not finishing my assignment? I was not well last night." Dad: "Sure I'll give you a note, John, but it mightn't say what you want." "What do you mean?" "Well, I'll say that in my view you didn't start work on the assignment soon enough and that this is why it isn't finished. It was due three days ago, after all. I'll also say, if you like, that your view is that you were too sick to finish it last night. Will that do?" John's reply: "Oh forget it!" "All right I will," says the father.

The tough part of consultancy is to pull back and to stay back even when we can see them walking into avoidable trouble. Nevertheless, unless safety is compromised, good consultant parents by and large restrict themselves to making observations and linking outcomes to previous activities or to poor planning.

> More on the homework: "I know you're upset, John. But, I don't have a lot of sympathy for you. You needed to work on this project days ago. I mentioned that to you at the time, you may remember. Had you done so, you wouldn't be in this position now. So really, this is a direct result of what you did and didn't do. I suggest you learn from this and act differently in future." The outcome: he was much more organized from then onward.

Even in the face of strenuous objections, this kind of thing is worth saying. When we do, we help to ensure that our teenagers make correct cause and effect connections. Also, remember that, when objecting intensely, they are taking in what we say more fully, not the opposite. We covered the value of resistance in Chapter 11.

Testing reality

Because seventeen-year-olds often naïvely romanticize or "catastrophize" about people, situations, and events, adults are important sounding boards for them. We can help them to develop more balanced views about things in several ways.

One way is simply to put different points of view, even in the face of stiff resistance. Mostly, this is a matter of stating what we think. Another option is to ask lots of questions, which are designed to stimulate thought. At times, this works well. However, at other times, they resist, all but saying, "Don't upset my hopes (or my miseries) by getting me to think sensibly!"

Should we meet persistent resistance, it is usually helpful to shift gears. We do this by getting them to express their feelings, which often does wonders by opening the floodgates. To encourage them, we simply make statements to them instead of asking them questions. (See ParentCraft *for more on this.) For example:*

★ *"You don't seem to like my questions."*

★ *"You seem upset."*

★ *"Tell me what you're feeling."*

★ *"You don't seem to want to consider someone else's views."*

★ *"What about telling me why this is so important to you."*

Each statement from us encourages them to vent their passions, worries, commitments, doubts, fears, and other feelings. Sometimes just repeating a single word is enough. Very soon we are likely to notice that they are calmer and more open to discussing things with us. They become more thoughtful, precisely because passion no longer holds sway inside them.

A common adult mistake is to think that all we need to do is to persist with our questioning like flies buzzing against a window! Unfortunately, this usually makes things worse, whereas helping them to discharge their feelings first commonly opens things up.

Clear "rules" about safety issues   Seventeen-year-olds still need plenty of input on safety at times. They have some big gaps and need our grown-up experience and alertness to fill those gaps in understanding. Even though they are now self-governing, we may need to take strong stands on certain issues to get them to take notice:

"No, it's not safe for you to come home alone at 11:00 p.m. on public transport. The city is unsafe for young women at that hour. I want you to get a taxi, ring me when you're ready to come home, and I'll come and get you or arrange for a friend to drive you. What will you do?"

If they persist in their plans, then we persist in talking to them about what they propose for as long as they will keep talking. While it does not always get them to change immediately what they propose, our persistence does have an impact. We may not see this for days, weeks, or months. It is sometimes only when they start to plan their lives differently by taking account of the safety issues we have raised, that we know that our persistence has been worth it. Our persistence also teaches them how to take a stand themselves.

Help to stand alone   Ensuring that our teenagers learn to take care of themselves effectively helps to ensure that they will stay safe as they venture into the world. At seventeen, many situations can arise in which their safety or welfare may depend on their determination and forthrightness. They need to learn to stand alone. We can help them to learn to do this by taking them through imaginary experiences, or by helping them to debrief after actual ones.

Think of the following situations related to driving:

★ The car driver is driving unsafely.

★ Passengers are distracting the driver.

★ Others are pressuring them to drink or do drugs.

★ Someone makes an unwelcome sexual advance.

We ask them what they think and, if necessary, give them specific coaching on what to do. Being specific is important. If it is an actual situation, congratulating them on what they did that worked is a useful first step. Suggesting some simple statements that they could use is very helpful to many young people too. For example:

★ "Slow down," "Drive safely," "Stop, I want to get out."

★ "I feel unsafe. Please stop shouting at Jim while he's driving."

★ "You drink it; I don't want it," "I'll have one later."

★ "No, I'm not willing to do that," "Go away," "Leave me alone."

Remember to introduce values and ethics regularly in these discussions. Here are some questions to start with:

★ What do you think is the best thing to do about this?

★ What kind of person would do that sort of thing?

★ Is that the kind of thing you want to support?

★ What do you think is the right thing to do in this kind of situation?

★ What will be the consequences to you as a person if you do that?

Thinking and planning for the future

Getting them thinking specifically about the future is useful. By this age, they need to begin at least to investigate what comes next for them. Some useful questions about jobs are:

★ *Do you know what you want to do with your life?*

★ *To what sort of work are you attracted?*

★ *Does the work you want to do require special training?*

★ *Do you want to go to college? If so, where?*

★ *How will you support yourself while studying?*

These are some questions about future living arrangements:

★ *Will you leave home at the end of school?*

★ *If so, how will you support yourself?*

★ *Are we willing to keep supporting you at home?*

★ *If you stay at home, what will we expect you to do?*

★ *Will we expect you to pay board? If so, about how much?*

What parents need

During this year, adults have another welcome respite. This offers the chance to connect or reconnect with young people through ease and harmony. Perhaps the biggest issue for most parents is having to watch "helplessly" as the young venture into the grown-up world.

To adjust to the change   Our children are very much easier to be with and, as in previous stages, we need to shift gears. It is very important that we notice the changes and respond to them. So, for example, when we "automatically" respond with the quick retort, or the inner sigh, or the impatient glance, or the "steeled and ready for battle" voice tone, we need to interrupt ourselves and act differently. Some people find it easier to do this if they imagine that they are talking to someone else's children. Parents can also help one another by agreeing to remind each other to act differently.

Managing our fears

Many "What if" questions arise, even plaguing some parents:

★   *What if they make mistakes?*

★   *What if they are at risk and get hurt?*

★   *What if something happens to them that we could have forseen?*

The reality is almost certainly that they will make mistakes, they will take risks, they will get hurt, they will provoke something that we could have foreseen, and more. The reality also is that we did, too, and we learned to live in the world. So why won't they?

What we now need to do is to face our fears. Our job with them is almost over; not over completely yet, but almost. So, for everyone's benefit, we need to adjust. Expressing our feelings to each other helps, as does talking to other parents whose children have already left home about how they managed and adjusted.

To begin to deal with the loss   At this stage, too, we often begin to miss them mightily. For seventeen years parents have usually had daily contact with their children. We have cared for them, guided them, loved them, kept them safe, and taken responsibility for ensuring that they grow up healthily and happily. The pleasure, fulfillment, and the meaning and purpose of these activities have added much of value to our lives. In fact, the same thing can be said of the experience of anyone who has devoted years to the care and nurture of children.

Now the writing is on the wall. We see much of this is coming to an end. Added to this, our teenagers start sharing lots with others that they used to share with us. They start to prefer their friends and future partners, and leave us out of the loop. The loss we feel when faced with this prospect is completely understandable.

Talking about the loss we are experiencing is important. By doing so, we learn increasingly to accept the reality of their impending departure. We also learn to let go of them and accept that they are now almost adults who will lead their own lives.

To discuss sexual issues   We may need to work out our position on sexual contact at home. We live in a time when young people are not unlikely to have intimate sexual contact when they are dating. Dealing with the various personal and family issues is important. Are we going to accept open kissing and cuddling when they are at home, or recommend privacy? What do we expect to happen when boyfriends or girlfriends stay the night? If they are sexually involved, do they sleep together? Or do we insist that they sleep apart? The values we hold as important will influence our answers to these kinds of questions, of course, and involving the young people in open discussion is imperative.

Ten easy things parents can do

1   Do companionable things together (such as shopping, walks, movies, or watching them play sports, dance, etc.).

2   Share family stories and history.

3   Celebrate their creativity.

4   Reality-test their romantic or catastrophic ideas.

5   Coach them to help them realize their dreams.

6   Thank them for their help around the home.

7   Read inspiring books or watch inspiring movies together.

8   Invite their friends home.

9   Tell them when we disagree with them.

10   Tell them that we won't desert them when they leave home.

Handy messages for seventeen-year-olds

★   "Hang in there. You can do it."

★   "What you're doing now is preparing you for the future. Your study/work/sport/. . . will make the rest of your life easier."

★   "Turn your dreams into reality by taking simple steps."

★   "If you have a big problem, break it up into manageable bits that you can solve."

★   "Help is available. Ask for it when you need it."

★   "Others probably feel like you."

★   "Stand your ground, say 'No,' set limits. You will gain other people's respect in this way, even if they criticize you now."

★   "Make sure that you are safe at all times. You are valuable. Look after yourself."

★   "Keep yourself safe. Remember to be sensible with alcohol and drugs, at parties and when driving. Your life can depend on what you do."

What parents say about seventeen-year-olds

Many parents really learn to enjoy their teenagers during this stage, one of the biggest challenges being letting go of them. Here is some of what they say.

Greatest pleasure

★　"their independence"

★　"the joy of watching a wonderful young adult unfold"

★　"their increased helpfulness at home"

★　"she was relaxed, friendly, and adult at times, and easier to talk to"

★　"her excitement about life, her strong opinions and values"

★　"his motivation to learn complicated computer procedures by himself."

Biggest challenge

★　"giving our daughters driving lessons!"

★　"keeping the family connections strong with our teenager wanting to go out more"

★　"letting the strings go quietly, while I still had some tied on for safety"

★　"getting her to stay at home during the week and do homework"

★　"feeling comfortable with them leaving the nest, even temporarily"

★　"worrying if they were safe and how they would manage the world"

★　"knowing when to exercise control and when to increase freedoms"

★　"having to accept that she could make big decisions about her own life."

Most needed

★ *"knowledge that the role of the parent becomes more collegial"*

★ *"[awareness] that the intensity of exchanges can be extreme and, at times, needs to be"*

★ *"[to know] how to assure my children that I loved them"*

★ *"[knowing whether to] drop all limits and how to let go while seeing the potential mistakes they could make"*

★ *"reassurance from parents with older children that all was going well."*

Big issues for seventeen-year-olds

The main focus for the "romantic" is dealing realistically with issues about the future and their expanding world.

Balancing realism with dreams

★ *learning to relish the wonder of dreams*

★ *discovering how to live practically not naïvely*

★ *learning to integrate feelings, thinking, and action, and that all three go together to support each other.*

Facing the future

★ *understanding that "the buck stops here"*

★ *realizing the implications of personal responsibility*

★ *discovering that responsibility requires their dealing with the consequences of their actions*

★ *dealing with their fears and hopes about the future*

★ *learning to ask for help when they need it*

★ *looking ahead, and facing and dealing with their fantasies of what it will mean to live "alone" outside the home*

★ *considering what their place in the world is going to be.*

Romantic relationships

★ practicing with partners

★ coming out as a couple in public—discovering what is involved

★ learning about commitment to one person, or more, and the implications of making and breaking these commitments

★ deciding what to do sexually

★ coping with the desire to spend special time with a boyfriend/girlfriend and balancing family and social life with these demands.

Big increase in workload

★ having to cope with the much greater demands at school or work

★ handling anxiety and other feelings about the extra demands they face in the next few years

★ facing the implications of what others say about the future without understanding from direct experience

★ committing, or otherwise, to our existing educational or other plans for them.

Managing the grown-up world

★ learning to set personal limits from within their own resources

★ asserting what is important to them with others and finding ways of pursuing their goals

★ understanding that results in life come from personal effort and action, and relishing this

★ realizing that they have more important learning to do and that parents can still help

★ fulfilling greater responsibilities at home.

CHAPTER 20

The world leader

(eighteen- to twenty-one-year-olds)

One day some friends of ours received a very formal request for an interview from their daughter's "world leader" boyfriend. It was just before Christmas. He arrived and told them very seriously that he was no longer a child and did not want anyone to give him Christmas stockings. He associated these gifts with being young and immature. Our friends said to us, "We associate them with sharing and fun." The outcome: they had fun as he watched.

At a parenting class, Wendy asked Ken about Philip, her "world leader" son. He refused to do his share of work at home. In the face of his "try and make me" stance, she had taken a strong position: either he did his share, or he had to leave and live somewhere else. His response was to leave. He went to live with family friends, whom he thought would demand less of him.

Through discussion with Ken, Wendy decided to write two letters, one to her friends and one to Philip. She sensitively suggested to her friends that she didn't think it was good for them to take in Philip under these circumstances. He had moved out to avoid doing legitimately assigned tasks at home. To Philip, she wrote that he was welcome to return home, provided that he pulled his weight completely from then on. Otherwise he was not welcome to live with her. She ended by wishing him well.

Later she wrote to Ken too. "I am writing to let you know how things worked out with Philip. I thought you might like to know that the situation was resolved. I wrote to Philip as you suggested and I also wrote a letter to my friends . . . Philip was back as soon as possible. He would have come home earlier if I had been there. He agreed to the conditions of my letter that he do his share. We had a long discussion about what this meant to us/him. Thanks very much for your help."

Eighteen- to twenty-one-year-olds in brief

Legally adults, these young people continue to grow in confidence during this three-year period. At the same time, this is often tempered by uncertainty about the future and doubts about the wider world.

The start   The "world leader" stage begins with a consolidation of previous patterns. The tentativeness of the "romantic" is often replaced with greater confidence and a real sense of self. "World leaders" often begin to weigh up their views on social conditions, the way the world operates, and justice and injustice. The morality and the rights and wrongs of all events may become the subject of passionate debate.

Central issue   A desire to contribute to the world is very important. Their ways of doing this are many, and their understanding of what is needed varies. They generally do want to make a difference. Their thoughts naturally turn to what lies ahead for them too. They often feel very uncertain about this, although some young people affect a beguiling certainty as they talk to adults. They are understandably preoccupied with the practicalities of finishing school or getting on at work. They are also intent on working out their values, and developing the spiritual dimensions of their lives can become a consuming interest.

Normal progress   Leaving home is natural at some time during this stage. Parents may now seem somewhat irrelevant emotionally as these young people start to commit to other people outside the family. Continuing as friendly consultants works particularly well if we cultivate respect for their privacy and their interests. When they get what they need, the stage passes with much shared satisfaction. If they don't, they may act with stormy forthrightness on almost everything.

The end   The end of this stage is when they complete the transition into adulthood. This is not necessarily accompanied by leaving home. In some parts of the world, the young stay at home until they finish their tertiary education. Nevertheless, if all has gone well, they are grown-ups and act like it. Of course, we hope to have friendly and mutually respectful relationships that will mature as the years pass. And we can have these when we *all* leave childhood behind us!

Celebrating our eighteen- to twenty-one-year-olds

Young people at this age are now very grown up and we can share adult pleasures with them as opportunities arise.

Enjoying their maturity   We still love them and can celebrate the emerging adults in all sorts of ways. To do this we may need to make ourselves available when they are. We may need to learn to make the most of the minutes they are with us, rather than continuing to rely on hours or days of contact. Doing this is worth it. Finding low-demand ways of making contact and keeping in touch is also helpful. Use these frequently. Acting like companions when with them and encouraging them to do the same with us often works well too.

Taking pride in their accomplishments   They are living their lives now and we have played an important part in that. We contributed to their formation. Our efforts helped to shape how they now live their lives, how centered they are in themselves, their sense of their own power, and how happy and fulfilled they are. We can notice all of this and pat ourselves on the back for our part in it. Parents, teachers, and friends can all discuss the contribution each has made. Of course, we may need to accept that their interests and accomplishments are different from what we expected or hoped for. We get a unique pleasure from recognizing them for themselves at this age.

Sharing them easily   When they form a relationship with someone, we can find ways of all sharing time enjoyably together. Many of them like to celebrate special events like birthdays, particularly the twenty-first, which is a very important "launching" event.

Enjoying their passion   If we remember when we were "world leaders" ourselves, we can enjoy the passion and the perceptiveness of these young adults. We can learn all sorts of things from them at this age, because they often see so clearly. Noticing what we agree with is important. At the same time, putting our points of view can contribute to wonderful debates. Discussing things respectfully and directly is very gratifying, both when we agree and when we disagree.

Inside our eighteen- to twenty-one-year-olds

"Dad," called Mikhail, "can you give me a hand in the garage?" "What are you doing?" "I'm fixing the car." "Okay," said Stefan, "I'll be there in five minutes." True to his word, Stefan appeared in the garage five minutes later dressed in his mechanic's clothes. "What do you need to do?" he asked as he walked in. "There's a problem with the fuel injection and I have to replace a small part." "Okay, show me what you're doing and what you want me to do to help." This occupied them for a few minutes. Then, as they got on with the job, Mikhail started to talk. "Dad, did you know that this tiny little part cost me hundreds of dollars. I just don't believe that it costs anywhere near that to produce. I think it's wrong to charge so much. And, you know what, I've found out that spare parts are marked up enormous amounts, some of my friends say as much as 300 percent. When I think of all the people like me who are trying to make ends meet on low wages, or others who are still at school, I really boil. It's not right! Something should be done to stop it." By this stage, Mikhail had stopped work and was waving his arms around to make his points. In measured tones, Stefan said, "I agree with you, son. Are you going to do something about it?" The work then proceeded side by side with sometimes passionate discussion of what to do.

"World leaders" are often both excited and frightened by the world waiting for them. Freedom is now almost completely within their grasp, yet there is so much to learn. They can fear or delight in doing all sorts of things that they have never done before. Also, feeling as grown up as they do often gives them pleasure. For example, driving a car for the first time alone, getting their first full-time job, going to college or the military, all can lift their spirits as they enjoy who they now are.

And, knowing that they can leave home at any time and that no one can stop them legally has a significant impact on many of them. Here is attractive freedom; here also is unknown, perhaps scary, territory.

Eighteen- to twenty-one-year-old upgrade

"World leaders" are reworking the experiences they had between ten and twelve years of age. Consistent with these ages, they often act assertively in ways designed to organize others and to change things around them. Nevertheless, their apparent certainty is often accompanied by significant anxiety.

Feelings   The push to take responsibility and to make a difference is deeply felt by many of them. "What am I to do with my life?" is an important question. Their interpretation of what is important varies enormously, as we would expect, from perhaps "the responsible citizen" to "the revolutionary." With many, the unpredictability of the world and worries about what could happen to them prompt them to feel for and find definite solutions. The meaning, purpose, fulfillment, and spirituality they find in these arise from their feelings.

Thinking   The "world leader," like the younger child he is upgrading, is very much a whole person. At this older age, they often think a great deal about social issues, as we have mentioned, and want to act effectively to change things. At the same time, they are naturally interested in their own lives. They can spend a great deal of time thinking about the pros and cons of the different life options, career choices, study routes, and work or non-work lifestyles available to them. Because they cannot yet see ahead and because they also feel young (ten to twelve years of age), they can engage in "endless," cyclic inner discussions. Gradually they learn, however, that only experience will teach them the certainty they crave.

Action   Again like ten- to twelve-year-olds, they often engage actively in social causes. When younger, issues in their immediate lives at home or school tended to dominate. However, at this age, their causes often have wider social implications like world peace or globalization. Based on their ethics and values, they may take to the streets, literally or figuratively, to make a stand. They often also feel a duty to act in all areas of their lives in ways that express openly their commitment to their own values, ethics, and spirituality.

What they're like for others

"Almost finished but not quite" sums up a great deal about "world leaders." They are now very close to being fully formed people. Yet they still have the finishing touches to add to what they have learned and they still have the new learning of this stage to do.

Trying to stand out   As they seek to form their own identities in the world, many of them seek to stand out from or against their origins. They seem to think that their independent identities will arise from a "not-orientation":

★ "I'm not like my parents."

★ "I'm not like my friends."

★ "I don't agree with globalization/abortion/whaling/..."

★ "I'm against working the way everyone else does."

While they learn many useful things in this way, eventually they need to work out that identity comes from discovering who they are, rather than who they are not. Until then, they can try the patience of adults and friends alike, particularly those whom they pull regularly into arguments about their pet issues.

Each generation seems to develop its own protest movements around which "world leaders" can polarize: anti-nuclear, pro-choice (abortion), anti-Vietnam War, gay and lesbian rights, anti-uranium mining, anti-abortion (we've come full circle), anti-globalization and anti-genetically engineered products.

Of course, some of them opt for conformity, cooperation, and identifying with the prevailing views of the communities in which they live. They seek actively to find themselves in relation to the context in which they grew, rather than by standing against them. These young people are often much more comfortable for others, particularly the older generations. However, and this is important, they are not necessarily going to discover themselves as fully as they could, were they to stand out from their context at least a little.

Challenging through their style   With their priority issues to the forefront, they act in whatever ways suit their passions and perceptions. Many styles are used to do this, including the conformist, drop-out, helpless victim, take-over merchant, predator, revolutionary, philosopher, sage, guru, missionary, good citizen, computer geek, sports jock, acolyte, convert, devotee, renegade, rebel, or terrorist. Clearly, some of their styles are easier to deal with than others.

Every act cries out, "This is who I am; I want you to honor me and my choices." Our responses to their cries are important.

Having "the answer"   Their answers are often different from the prevailing ones, which is potentially helpful and educational, and potentially irksome. A lot depends on the stances they adopt along the way. Those who adopt "know it all" or "there's something wrong with you if you disagree with me" stances are often difficult to deal with.

Often "right" and "wrong"   Uncluttered by grown-up experiences and commitments, "world leaders" often see right through the blind spots of their elders. The accuracy of their perceptions, in itself, is often hard to manage.

Our challenge is to remain open to our "world leaders" and what they're saying when lifetimes of effort and endeavor are accurately described as creating problems, out of date, or no longer worth considering.

The truth usually is, however, that they both see clearly and do not see everything. With practice and determination, we can learn to affirm their clarity and avoid retreating into finding fault. With this advance, we can often create opportunities to highlight the wisdom that is embedded in what they may feel inclined to discard completely.

What eighteen- to twenty-one-year-olds need

Whether still students, working, unemployed, or doing other things, "world leaders" need to deal with a big expansion of their worlds and all the changes that this carries with it. They are now rapidly approaching full emotional adulthood and so are given and take much more freedom and responsibility. Those still at school have all the extra pressures of final year examinations and assessments. They also need to decide what comes next: more study, work, or something else. Many young people leave home at some stage during this period and they have lots to learn as they do.

Back-up   Faced with their maturity, we may miss how much they still need the backing of adults who care about them. Many of them are involved in activities that require persistence, organization, application, and commitment. As with many adults, their motivation and commitment, and how well they apply themselves, can vary greatly. Also, they do not suddenly grow out of all the inner turbulence that can cloud their judgement or pull them off course.

Parents and other adults who are available and open to discussion can provide much needed support. Some teenagers cannot do without it. All the same, we are wise to remember that we are increasingly becoming optional extras in their lives.

Continued contact   Once their children get to eighteen or more years of age, many parents think that they can cope without much contact. Many also think that it is intrusive or interfering for us to keep in touch. However, the sudden change from family life, with its predictable routines and ways of doing things, to the openness of life "alone" is too much for lots of teenagers to manage without considerable stress.

Some do cope well, of course. Unfortunately, many do not. They lose direction, become significantly anxious or depressed, or begin to behave erratically. Some get caught up in styles of life that are not good for them—not eating or sleeping well, smoking marijuana or doing other drugs, not paying bills, or giving up work or study.

Young people are more likely to stay on track if Mom and Dad, or some other caring adults, are active in the background as an interested, supporting presence. The way this works is that the repeated contacts act as unstated reminders of the values and standards of behavior that the young people have learnt when growing up.

For "world leaders" who have just left home, we recommend daily contact, even if it's only for a few seconds. Longer is possible, too, of course. Here is a sample of our side of a brief conversation:

"Hi. Just want to see how you are."

"Everything's okay."

"Good. Contact us if you need anything."

"Okay. Love you. Bye."

We gradually decrease the number of times we initiate contact as they get older and more accustomed to living alone. Interestingly, contact frequently continues, sometimes regularly, sometimes less so, well into their twenties, when it is often initiated by them.

Information and discussion   Our regular contact with them gives them access to a wealth of information about coping practically with the world. After leaving home, they will have to do many things for the first time, like arranging and paying for services (gas, electricity, telephone), signing leases, and paying their rent on time. Having us there to make suggestions and to talk about their options is often helpful.

This is a very rewarding time for many parents and their children. A great sense of mutuality is possible and this develops increasingly through these years as we discuss lots of things. Our grown-up children naturally and increasingly define themselves as our colleagues and equals, particularly if we encourage this in the way we act with them. Doing so makes many new and different types of satisfaction possible. For example, the bogey of suddenly finding ourselves cast in the role of restrictive mom or dad tends to fall away.

Common questions for discussion

★ Do I need to insure my things?

★ Where can I get a good deal on electrical goods?

★ Do you know a good bank that could give me a personal loan?

★ What is the best way to organize the telephone and other bills when living in a shared house?

★ What do I do if roommates start to do drugs or other things that I disagree with?

★ How can I get my roommates to keep shared areas neat and tidy?

To decide to stay or to go As we have already mentioned, leaving home at this age is natural. However, many factors come into whether or not our young do go. For example, unemployment, college studies, the expense of living away from home, a young person's unreadiness to leave, or a desire to have all the services of home still supplied may induce some to want to stay at home. By contrast, factors such as having to live away from home to do certain courses or types of work, not getting along well with the family, a desire for independence, or attractive opportunities to live alone or with others may encourage some to leave.

Of course, in one sense, the decision to stay or to go is not theirs alone. We need to be involved, since the homes they will leave or stay in are ours. Also, some of them need us to take a clear stand and urge strongly one way or the other, depending on their abilities.

Generally, we suggest fostering an attitude of patient openness through the process. Our openness communicates both acceptance of their leaving and encouragement for them to do so. Patience is needed because they often swing back and forth between "I'm leaving" and "I'm staying" until they finally decide. Then, too, once gone, they may want to return for a while, only to leave again later.

The process seems to go more easily for many families when we set clear guidelines about how we want them to approach these issues. For example, in the face of attempts to get us to argue to stop them leaving, we may assert, "Go. By all means go. We think it's wonderful that you want to go. You don't have to create a fight or a rift to do it. Leave with our blessing. And when you go, remember that we are here for you, if you need us."

To contribute if staying   We strongly recommend that those who stay have full adult responsibilities in the home. This means their doing all that they would have to do for themselves if they had left, including housekeeping, paying their own costs, doing home maintenance, cooking, and washing.

The many advantages of this approach include:

★ They are much less likely to treat home as a dormitory or hotel.

★ Paying helps the budget and teaches them financial responsibility.

★ They are encouraged to leave because they aren't living in a fully serviced hotel and their freedom will beckon.

★ It prepares them for coping "alone" when they do leave.

★ They develop much more respect for the other adults at home.

You may need determination for this and, at times, ingenuity. For example, some of them use staying out late or the pressure of other activities as excuses not to fulfill their duties. Here is a wonderfully creative parental solution to get a twenty-year-old son to do his chores.

After repeated discussions about doing the dishes on his rostered nights, Robert still stayed out late and "just didn't seem to get around to doing them." This left his parents with the job every time. Realizing that they were much more uncomfortable about the outcome than he was, they worked out how to shift the discomfort to him. The next night that he failed to do the dishes as agreed, he got home late to discover all the unwashed dishes in his bed. He was outraged, but he did his share from then on. Interestingly, he also left home a few months later.

To declare themselves   At this age, young people are in the process of establishing themselves in the world on their own feet and in their own ways. As part of this, they may make "extreme" personal declarations to adults who are important to them. In effect, they are saying, "This is who I am. I want you to honor me." Some clearly select their new identities because they know that they will shock. They provocatively challenge us to accept or reject them:

★ "What about this one?"

★ "Do you really mean that you accept who I am?"

★ "Can I really live my own life?"

Our best response to these declarations is honesty. If we agree with them, that is wonderful. We can share this and celebrate with them:

"Let's see if I understand this. You're telling us that you're a radical, pacifist, whale-loving, gay/lesbian, anti-globalization, radical pro-choice environmentalist. Have we got that right? Yes. Oh well, that all seems fairly straightforward."

However, we may have reservations, even significant disagreements. Then the question is how to tell them this directly and openly. Some adults find doing so a big challenge. We sense that our young crave our automatic agreement, understanding, and acceptance and, preferably, want us to join in fully by embracing with equal enthusiasm whatever they have embraced. Not doing so will, it can seem to us, cause disappointment or worse.

Nevertheless, we still recommend open discussion. They need our honesty. Also, if we pretend, they usually know that we are faking it and we will lose respect in their eyes. To add to the challenge at times, too, our disagreeing can prompt vigorous assertions that our opinions are unacceptable or flawed, perhaps even that we are too. If they do respond like this, they need us to engage, just as vigorously if necessary, to seek their respect as they talk to us:

"Yes, I disagree with you. That doesn't make either of us bad. You are living your own life, deciding who you're going to be and what you're going to do. They're important choices and they're yours—not mine. It's your life. You don't have to make me wrong for you to be right. I would like you to accept us both as okay, talk respectfully, and test the validity of your ideas through your own experiences, not by fighting us. I support you in this."

Respect as adults   They need adults to respect them. They also need to adjust to perceiving themselves as adults. The respect that we and other grown-ups show them is a powerful help to them in making this adjustment. Our actions will usually be welcome, too, because at this age they are often very aware of personal dignity and self-esteem.

Simple ways to show adult respect to "world leaders"

★ *When talking about plans, comments like, "You may already have your own plans," or questions like, "Have you already made plans for . . .?" help to highlight respect.*

★ *If they are at home, we can knock before entering their rooms, or ask through the door, "May I come in?"*

★ *If they live in their own home, we can ask permission before we go to another room: "Is it all right if I use your toilet?" or "May I go into the kitchen and get a glass?"*

★ *When arranging to visit, we can ask, "Is it convenient for you for us to visit you on/at ...?"*

★ *On the telephone, we can ask, "Is now a good time to talk?"*

Acceptance of partners   Young people are often pairing off by this time. They are learning about emotional closeness and physical intimacy in close relationships. It can be a lovely time, particularly when they feel very loving towards one another. Our responses to this are significant and we need to make them with sensitivity to their likely responses to us. What we think usually matters a lot, even if they declare otherwise.

Guidelines about partners

★ *Genuine interest in their partners is great.*

★ *Reserving judgment and allowing plenty of time for everyone to get to know one another in the beginning removes all sorts of pressures.*

★ *Finding ways of welcoming them to, and including them in, family activities is important.*

★ *Looking for opportunities to spend relaxed, casual time with couples usually pays off.*

★ *Polite acceptance, if we are uncomfortable with a partner, is generally better than withdrawal or antagonism.*

★ *Expressing doubts or trying to influence them against partners usually strengthens their bonds with each other "against us."*

★ *Setting limits on behavior in our own home remains an option with partners, as it is with any other adult visitor who acts inappropriately.*

A send-off celebration   Giving them a party or some other send-off helps to mark their transition into full adulthood. Psychologically and emotionally this is important. They need us to celebrate their having reached adulthood, to acknowledge their new mature status publicly. They need us to declare our love for them as grown-up members of the family. A twenty-first birthday party can do all of this.

What parents need

Our primary need is to learn to let go and to celebrate their maturity and, when they do, their leaving home. Previously, when our young people left the nest, we knew that they were going to return. At this age, however, they are readying themselves to leave permanently.

To deal with the loss   When our children spread their wings and fly off, we have losses to deal with. As parents we feel this keenly; so do our friends and our other children. Everyone else who has taken a strong interest in them—teachers, custodial workers, youth workers— is also likely to feel at least some loss.

> ### *Grieving the departure of our young adults*
>
> *To deal with our feelings of loss, it is important that we discuss how we feel, the differences their departures have made to our lives, the things that we used to enjoy about them and what we now miss. Allowing whatever time this takes is important. With some young people we can adjust quickly. With others it takes much longer—perhaps even years. Of course, if we continue to have contact of some sort, then the loss is often not as great. However, a complete cut is like a kind of death that generally results in the need for much more grieving.*

To find something else to do   Parents or caretakers who have devoted most of their time to raising the departing young people will benefit from filling their lives with other things. Many have big holes to fill. To do this may require deliberate thought and action. A few ideas include joining clubs, going back to work or working longer, starting a course of study, or spending more time with friends.

To let go   It seems so easy to say, but the reality of letting go of young people whom we have nurtured for years is a great challenge for many people. However, we need to find ways of doing it, as they are now grown up and are living their own lives. The danger of not doing so can mean losing or distancing our children because of our possessiveness or intrusiveness.

At the point when their son was about to get married, one mother and father behaved very strangely. Because these parents lived a long way from where the wedding was to be, they arranged to stay with the couple, who were already living together. The astounding part of the arrangement was that they stayed for one week before the wedding and two weeks afterward. The parents were apparently completely unaware of the intrusiveness of this.

To share our success with others   We are now at the end of the process. It is time for a celebration of what we have achieved. If we have not celebrated at all yet, then these celebrations are long overdue.

To celebrate, we can share lots of memories from the twenty-one years we have devoted to each of our children. It is wonderful to talk to each other about the things we have enjoyed and to congratulate each other on the achievement. Here are some areas to share:

★ the qualities of these young adults that we applaud

★ what we are proud of in them

★ what we admire in each other that contributed to their development

★ particular challenges that we met successfully

★ the joy of seeing how they are now living.

Ten easy things parents can do

1   Listen to them when they want to talk about things that are troubling them.

2   Take an interest in their study, work, and other activities.

3   Applaud their successes and comment on their maturity.

4   Talk animatedly about their interests, tapping into their excitement to do so if we aren't spontaneously excited.

5   Go out together to "grown-up" places; take their friends.

6   Discuss the state of the world and "what needs to change."

7   Accept that they think and feel as they express themselves.

8   Express our opinions clearly, and stand our ground when we disagree if necessary.

9   Talk to other adults about what we like and are proud of.

10   Keep in daily touch by visiting, phone, fax, email, or letter.

Handy messages for eighteen- to twenty-one-year-olds

★   *"You are in charge now. You're responsible for yourself."*

★   *"I'm/We're proud of you."*

★   *"We want you to have a wonderful life."*

★   *"I don't have to be wrong for you to be right."*

★   *"If you stay at home, you'll have an adult share to do."*

★   *"We are still here for you. Just because you've left doesn't mean we've rejected you."*

★   *"Make sure you look after yourself well—eat, rest, exercise— do all the right things."*

★   *"It's a trade. Our continuing to do what we do to support you depends on you doing your part by . . . ."*

★   *"Hang in there. The answers you want will come with more experience. Keep going."*

What parents say about eighteen- to twenty-one year-olds

The goal is to encourage our grown-up children to go out into the world and, at the same time, to maintain close friendships with them. Here is what some parents have said about this stage.

Greatest pleasure

★ *"the sense of achievement [we had] that they had grown up, were happy and doing well"*

★ *"seeing them blossom and make good new friends"*

★ *"lots of good things all coming to fruition"*

★ *"learning to care for their own health"*

★ *"studying and being self-disciplined"*

★ *"their independence and us having a parental role"*

★ *"their excitement about life"*

★ *"relating to them in the role of a supportive friend"*

★ *"her warm 'adult' connections to us as people and as parents"*

★ *"signs and gestures of appreciation from them for our efforts."*

Biggest challenge

★ *"letting go and not giving advice, unless asked or it was really needed"*

★ *"not being around to protect/care for her"*

★ *"standing back and trusting them to manage their own lives"*

★ *"saying 'Goodbye' as he left home and not seeing him so much"*

★ *"worrying about what was really going on at times"*

★ *"their seeming sometimes like strangers"*

★ *"maintaining expectations of how this young adult should contribute to the household."*

Most needed

★ *"[assurance] that she could look after herself and stay safe"*

★ *"[assurance] that keeping close, daily contact with her at the start of the separation was needed and wanted by her"*

★ *"to know how to act as a persuasive friend without taking charge"*

★ *"to know how to set guidelines for what young adults could do at home"*

★ *"to save advice for when they were willing to absorb it."*

Big issues for eighteen- to twenty-one-year-olds

For our young people this is a period of real discovery—about themselves and about the world—so most of their challenges emanate from finalizing the process of becoming mature adults living in an adult world.

Dealing with expanded worlds

★ *handling study and exams and managing the pressures of finishing school*

★ *dealing with starting jobs or college studies*

★ *completing and rounding out their personal development*

★ *learning to relate to a wide range of people*

★ *accepting other people from many different backgrounds.*

Developing intimate relationships

★ *developing or exploring emotional and possibly physical intimacy with partners*

★ *discovering how to maintain intimacy over an extended period*

★ *learning to solve problems with partners*

★ *possibly setting up house with partners.*

Leaving or staying home

★ deciding with parents about going or staying

★ negotiating this with all involved

★ discovering that their parents are people

★ leaving or staying in ways that affirm and accept everyone

★ remaining available to consultation with adults as needed

★ finding some form of financial support

★ handing in the door key

★ managing themselves with alcohol, drugs, driving, and sex.

Contributing to their support systems

★ contributing financially to their families if at home, or to their own households if they have left

★ doing their share of what is necessary where they live

★ taking initiative to improve living arrangements.

Learning about the world

★ learning how to set up house

★ managing their own affairs "alone"

★ recognizing when they need help and finding out who to ask

★ discovering the various important practical issues to deal with regularly: bill-paying, insurance, cooperation with other householders, paying and retrieving bonds on rented accommodation, and so on

★ managing "alone" without parents or family immediately available.

Finding a meaningful place in the world

★ Answering the questions: "Who am I?" "What is important to me in this life?" "What will I do that will express who I am?" "How can I live so that I experience what I do as meaningful?"

★ Accepting "This is my life."

Epilogue:
Three final remarks

Now that you are at the end of the book, we remind you of how we have already suggested you use its contents. Throughout, we have described teenage patterns, issues, and needs in "pure form." We did this to assist your understanding of what we have repeatedly observed are the essential elements in the lives of teenagers at different stages. However, and this is very important, descriptions of generalities do not describe our children; there is very much more to them.

Our children are each the way each of them is. Some will show many of the qualities we have described, some will not. Some will show the qualities directly, some indirectly. Some will mix qualities from different ages into a mishmash that can make it difficult for us to identify clearly what they are dealing with. Even so, whatever the reality of each of our children, one thing needs to remain clear to us.

Our teenagers need us to relate to, plan for, care about and love them the way they are, and not to try to fit them or force them into anyone else's descriptions. Accordingly, we recommend that you only use the material that is helpful and that you put the rest aside.

The second point we want to make is to be persistent in problem-solving. Over the years, we have concluded that this is one of the most useful qualities for parents to cultivate for, as we have discovered, so much is dependent on it.

All problems can be solved. Just because we do not have the answer right now does not mean that there is no answer, only that we have not found it yet. To succeed, all we need to do is to persist in the search for solutions and in trying out the things that seem promising, even if the process takes a long time.

Finally, the fulfillment and many of the joys and satisfactions that can accompany life with our teenagers are potentially available to us all. We hope that what you have read here contributes in at least some small measure to your having these in full measure.

Authors' notes

Page viii ". . . *ParentCraft: A practical guide to raising children well* **has many important suggestions . . . that are very helpful in raising teenagers."** Published by Finch Publishing, Sydney, 2001. Excellent advice is also available in Michael Carr-Gregg & Erin Shale, *Adolescence: A guide for parents,* Finch Publishing, Sydney, 2002.

Page 14 "Dealing with the challenge" We have presented many useful tips that can help you juggle these demands in *ParentCraft.*

Page 19 "That [teenagers'] regrowth followed the same sequence as children grow through in their first twelve years was also obvious." See *ParentCraft,* Chapter 21.

Page 19 ". . . a summary in the *New Scientist* [had] some very exciting research findings into children's brain development": "Teen angst rooted in busy brain," *New Scientist,* vol. 176, issue 2365, 2002, p. 16, and "Rebels with a cause," *New Scientist,* vol. 165, issue 2222, 2000, p. 22. You will find further reading in Elizabeth R. Sowell and others, "In vivo evidence for post-adolescent brain maturation in frontal and striatal regions," *Nature Neuroscience,* vol. 2, 1999, p. 859, and Jay Giedd and others, "Brain development during childhood and adolescence: a longitudinal MRI study," *Nature Neuroscience,* vol. 2, 1999, p. 861.

Page 20 ". . . repetition is important here. It is through this that the necessary nerve fibers are formed and consolidated": Ken came across the rewiring potential in both adults and children when in the early 1970s he used what were then called "repatterning" exercises, which were designed to compensate for or fill in the gaps in people's neurological networks. Developed by Glenn Doman and Carl Delacato, repetition was fundamental to these.

At the time, the approach and the claims that repatterning could occur through exercise were very controversial. Nevertheless, Ken used the exercises with schizophrenic people with whom he was working and observed some very interesting changes in their inner stability, sense of self, and their capacity to make decisions. The exercises he used were outlined in Carl H. Delacato, *A New Start for the Child with Reading Problems: A manual for parents,* David McKay Company, New York, 1970.

More recently, Christopher Reeve, of *Superman* fame, has been using a repetitive approach to rewiring his spine since he became a quadriplegic. He has had some small and exciting success to date. And for decades, it has been common practice to give stroke victims repetitive exercise routines to help them to reprogram their brains to recover bodily functions (like moving an arm) that were lost due to brain damage from the stroke.

In relation to teenagers, we are claiming that the principle holds true for those areas of the brain to do with social awareness and judgment, decision-making, and planning.

Page 23–24 "It is the force behind the unfolding miracle of life that we can observe in our children": Many sciences and traditions have referred to this vital force for thousands of years. It is called by many names, including "chi," "shakti," "life force," "orgone," and "life energy." Western empirical science has recently "discovered" it and is now experimenting to find out how it works and what it contributes to us. Many scientists increasingly say that the "spiritual schools" of the East have for thousands of years taught the truth and value of what they are now discovering through Western empirical means.

Page 24 "People in their late twenties to mid-thirties and in their early to late forties are generally inwardly directed": The "mid-life crisis" that many people live through in their early forties is to do with a shift into a "breathing in" phase. It can be aggravated by resisting the pull to go inwards. Those who try to "force the pace" in their lives tend to "resist" the pull to go inside. To keep forcing, however, is a path to burn-out, ill health, and premature death when acted out in the extreme.

These days, the busy workers who won't allow themselves to change style and slow down as their system moves through these cycles frequently end up collapsing under the strain. The "breathing in" phases are important rest periods in our lives. We need them to enable us to maintain balance and to prepare us for the next outward phase. Looking at the increasing numbers of people who are "dying young" from overwork is a salutary reminder. The human body is not a machine. We need to treat our bodies as the living organisms they are with rhythms that ebb and flow as a natural part of how they maintain themselves—and us.

Page 24 "Young adults in their early to late twenties and older adults from their mid-thirties to early forties generally thrive on the 'busyness' of life . . .": As with the inward phase, there are those in the outward phase who resist following the outward flow of their energy, particularly those previously inclined to doing little. Interestingly, inactivity can create as many problems, although generally different ones, as being overly busy. Withholding full expression for the urge to become active and involved can result in mild to severe depression, or ill health from under-exercise.

Doing this can also lay the foundation for anxiety, possibly even panic attacks, from the build-up of vital force in our system that results. This can make us feel like pressure cookers. Our systems are designed for activity and without it they lose equilibrium very quickly. It is, of course, a matter of balance. Overdoing the expressiveness, as mentioned in the previous note, can lead to problems too.

Page 27 "Notice, too, the transition at the end of the teenage years": The cycle and these transitions keep occurring for the whole of our lives. You can work out for yourself where you are currently in your life (in an inward or outward phase, or going through a transition from one to the other).

Page 28 "Uncomfortable experiences are, in fact, fairly common [during transitional periods]": The patterns among adults are very much the same as those of teenagers.

When moving from an active, outwardly directed phase to a receptive, inwardly directed phase, the issues are to do with whether we have any fundamental value as people, whether what we have done so far has any meaning, whether we have wasted our time to

this point in our lives or have got everything wrong, whether it is worth continuing to live or better to die, whether we are worth anyone else taking an interest in us, or whether to commit suicide or to keep struggling and try harder to become a better person.

These transitions arise at 13–14, 27–28, 41–42, 55–56, 69–70, 83–84, 97–98 . . . years of age.

When the move is from a receptive, inwardly directed phase to an active, outwardly directed phase, the issues are to do with self-worth in relation to the value of the world, the value of the contribution we can make to the world, experiencing an inability to make a worthwhile contribution, or feeling troubled by not being able to see ahead to what is important and how to achieve that. Other issues may arise too, of course.

These transitions arise at 6–7, 20–21, 34–35, 48–49, 62–63, 76–77, 90–91 . . . years of age.

Page 30 "Hear them out and encourage them to express themselves—even their intense feelings." See *ParentCraft*, Chapters 13, 14, and 15 for some ways of doing this.

Page 31 "All the same, continue to express your views with 'I-statements,' such as those above." See also *ParentCraft*, p. 72.

Page 33 ". . . during the teenage years they revisit each developmental stage that they went through from conception to late childhood": You will find a summary of these stages in *ParentCraft*, Chapter 21.

Page 33 "As [babies] grow, they gradually become more mobile, physically capable, aware of other people . . .": The various aspects of these developments and the stages through which babies grow are summarized in *ParentCraft*, Chapter 21.

Page 36 "At about thirteen, teenagers revisit their baby years . . . At about fourteen, they revisit the two-year-old period": This period enables them to modify the outcomes that arose during their emotional births as children. It also helps them to modify the outcomes of their physical births as babies. All three are often connected. The physical lays the foundation for the emotional and usually has a stronger binding influence on later development. Similarly, the emotional lays the foundation for the cognitive and usually has a stronger binding influence on development that comes afterwards. So the physical birth is usually the most influential, the emotional birth the next most influential, and the cognitive birth comes next.

Page 43 "Very importantly, fathers and others present can also bond during this time": Historically, fathers were not encouraged to be present at the birth of their children in most Western countries. It was women's and doctors' business and fathers were kept out. They were often portrayed as figures of fun whose main function was to pace up and down outside closed doors during the delivery and to hand out cigars at the end. This has changed a lot in recent times. Fathers are now able to participate in the births of their children and so involve themselves in the bonding process. Our experience is that fathers who bond with their children at the birth remain much more naturally "connected" with them than those who do not. We highly recommend it to everyone.

Page 52 "… when we start to look into it, we find a great variety of opinions, many of which conflict": Very interestingly, some approaches to dealing with teenagers keep emerging year after year and these warrant investigation as they have stood the test of time. In fact, modern Western psychology has been around for over one hundred years and many methods have been researched and tested.

While repeated use of something over the years adds weight to its usefulness, we need to stay alert for flaws. Just because parents do something in a particular way over generations does not necessarily mean that it is a good thing. Think of how spanking, hitting, and beating children were routinely considered part of "good parenting." "Spare the rod and spoil the child" was still a common statement up to the early fifties in some areas. In fact, some schools still have a caning policy. However, we now know that hitting, spanking, and other ways of abusing children harm them. They are wounded by this kind of thing and the wounds remain with them long into the future.

At the same time as questioning established practice to ensure that it is

worthwhile and effective in the modern world, another form of caution is also important. In the world as it is today, new things often attract people simply because they are new. It often seems that, if they can help us to avoid difficulty or to meet challenges easily, they are even more attractive to lots of people. And, of course, this makes sense. Many advances have been made by people coming up with new approaches, which have been of great benefit to the world.

However, the newness or popular appeal of an approach to raising and managing children does not of itself make it right, safe, or good for them. Many fads promising simple answers and easy pathways to success have resulted in serious consequences for our children that were unnoticed at the time, only to appear as the years have passed. The problems arise usually because such fads are based on oversimplification of what is occurring and do not pay enough attention to the balance of forces in operation.

Examples of such fads include:

- Raising children permissively is best— they don't need clear limits and guidelines.
- Children should be allowed to choose what they eat on the assumption that they intuitively know what they need.
- Children can be passed to other people to raise without it having any effect on them.
- Attention deficit and hyperactivity disorder (ADHD), once popularly (not technically) known as hyperactivity and then as attention deficit disorder (ADD), is purely a dietary problem or a brain condition, and not something that child-rearing can affect.
- Parents can pull back from their teenagers, as they have grown up sufficiently to manage themselves.

Page 52 ". . . rupturing parent–child bonds prematurely is profoundly disturbing for the young": We have worked as psychotherapists and counselors for over thirty years. Every time the parent–child bond has been broken prematurely in the lives of our clients, they experienced disturbance that significantly influenced their later lives. Whether adopted at birth or later, fostered, sent to boarding school, neglected, abused, rejected, or ignored, they all paid a very big price. Teenagers whose parents don't keep the necessary contact with them are as prone to producing these effects as neglectful parents are on younger children. To us, these results speak for themselves.

Page 53 "Given their need for their parents, it is little wonder that the safest, least at risk teenagers are usually well engaged with their parents": Children and parents who bonded well in the earlier years usually seem to stay engaged more easily in the teenage years. They already have a basic connection. When early bonding has not gone well, we can still do lots to get engaged. Powerful bonds arise naturally, simply through doing things together day after day, year after year. Add passionate exchanges from time to time, both of delight and discomfort, and connections between parents and children generally become even stronger. Think of solid friendships between people as examples of how this can work.

Page 63 "When lives or property are significantly threatened, find ways to take over—and do it by force if necessary": We have always found the police very good when called in to help. They can support parents in getting back control of a situation at home where teenagers are escalating out of control. It is helpful to explain to the police what is happening and what you want them to help with.

Just the appearance of police uniforms at the door is often sobering enough to bring calm to a situation. A visit to the sergeant for a talk about the consequences of certain actions can also have a positive effect on young people.

Crisis Assessment Teams, or similar, can be very effective in helping to manage teenagers in a crisis. These are mental health teams attached to local areas that deal with mental health emergencies 24 hours a day, 7 days a week. Anyone can call. An assessment will be done on the telephone to decide if the police are needed, if the team needs to attend immediately, or if an appointment in the near future with a professional helper is all that is necessary.

Seeking the help of friends is part of the "tough love" approach too. Clearly, this kind of thing is very relevant for protection from young people who resort to physical violence regularly. They find out that acting violently results in their having to deal with a group of adults intent on stopping them. It helps to communicate the adult world's position to them very clearly. Those involved may need to become very verbally forceful, too, when young people use violence. If they find that they have to deal with a number of adults who are united in their position on violence, then the young people are more likely to take in, and adapt to, what is being said and expected of them. Of course, violence by parents toward their children is completely counterproductive—and illegal.

The courts can be asked to issue an Intervention Order, or similar, on children who are assaulting or menacing their parents. The children continue to live at home, but have to meet certain requirements of behavior set by the court. If these are broken, the court is then brought back into the situation and decides what will be done. The whole process of going in front of a judge and having formal orders issued has a very sobering effect on some young people. There are examples of teenagers behaving very badly with their single parents (mothers or fathers) who have transformed their behavior overnight through this approach.

Page 64 "Books like *ParentCraft* or *Adolescence: A guide for parents* . . . contain all sorts of ideas about achievable outcomes": See Further Reading, page 209 for publishing details.

Page 64 ". . . if our teenagers favor bullying tactics, we can get all sorts of strategies from a wonderful book called *Bully Busting* by Evelyn Field": Evelyn M. Field, *Bully Busting: How to help children deal with teasing and bullying*, Finch Publishing, Sydney, 1999. The title may mislead you because of its reference to children. However, for years we have recommended this book to adults who have been bullied by other adults or by their children. Many have freed themselves as a direct result of what they have read in this book.

Page 64 "If you have little self-confidence, then consider getting professional help to develop it": Some people are reluctant to seek professional help because they feel embarrassed, or they think they should know how to help themselves, or they just don't want to for some other reason. Thinking of getting help as the equivalent of going to a doctor when we are unwell or getting a plumber when the pipes need attention will help. And remember the consequences for our children and ourselves if we don't. Seeking expert help when we need to is a very wise thing to do, particularly these days when so much competent help is available.

Page 64 ". . . two very informative books on what is called 'tough love'": Phyllis and David York and Ted Wachtel, *Toughlove*, Bantam Books, New York, 1983, and Phyllis and David York and Ted Wachtel, *Toughlove Solutions: Runaways, Sex, Suicide, Drugs, Alcohol, Abuse, Disrupted Families, Community Indifference*, Bantam Books, New York, 1985.

Page 76 "Others have described this time as a roller coaster ride . . .": Michael Carr-Gregg and Erin Shale, *Adolescence: A guide for parents*, Finch Publishing, Sydney, 2002.

Page 82 "We identify six different teenage stages": You will find another presentation of these stages in Ken and Elizabeth Mellor, *ParentCraft: A practical guide to raising children well*, 2nd ed., Finch Publishing, Sydney, 2001. We were introduced to the notion that there are six stages by Jacqui Schiff, with whom Ken trained in the early 1970s. Others in the field of Transactional Analysis were also thinking along these lines at the time. More recently, the main approach of a number of authors has been to divide adolescence into three stages: the beginning, the middle, and the end. We think, however, that the changes teenagers make are more varied than this and that there are many advantages in a more detailed division.

Page 89 "... what does not work is to ... imagine something is wrong and get professional help when it is not needed": The vast majority of young people going through this stage need good parenting, not therapy. They need their parents available to them, perhaps intensely. When parents are available, young people will generally grow through the stage and arrive in good shape at the next one. True, a minority of young people may have severe psychological problems and need professional help. However, we emphasize that this is a very small minority.

Page 91 "Accepting young people fully at this age has the further benefit of healing many old hurts and emotional injuries from their baby years": Most, probably all people, reach adulthood with unmet needs. This is normal. Parents contribute to this outcome. However, we are not to blame. Yes, we play a part in producing their problems, but we are not solely responsible. Also, in mentioning old hurts and emotional injuries, we are not suggesting neglect or abuse by most parents. Nevertheless, neglect or abuse inflicted on children does create deep wounds that would not otherwise arise. Parents who do this kind of thing are responsible and need to do all they can to solve whatever problems they have that prompt them to act as they do. Getting professional help is imperative.

Page 115 "As young people adapt to the expectations and limits we set, they learn how to take control of themselves . . . if your teenager is a genius or severely challenged, we suggest that you do even more than normal to get them to learn these lessons": Without these skills, people don't learn the self-discipline necessary to take advantage of their own talents or of external opportunities as they arise. The number of very talented people like this is huge: painters, computer specialists, athletes, scientists, writers, mathematicians. They do not have enough self-discipline, for example, to get out of bed on time, to persist with a long-term task, or to resist acting on the impulse to smoke marijuana.

Similarly, people with physical or intellectual handicaps also need to learn to adapt to expectations and limits. Many people think this is not possible, even today. However, virtually all children can learn, provided we find humane ways of having an impact on them and persisting until they do learn. For example, people with Down's Syndrome were routinely put in institutions during the twentieth century on the grounds that it was the most humane practice available. These days, they are encouraged to do whatever they are capable of doing—even completing university studies, which some have.

Page 189 "Many young people leave home at some stage during this period": This is not true in all countries, or in all groups within the U.S. In Germany, for example, adult children often stay at home until they have finished college study, being well into their twenties before they leave.

Acknowledgments

In many ways, producing this book has been a team effort. Unfortunately, space does not allow us to mention everyone by name. Nevertheless, we have highly valued all contributions.

Jacqui Schiff, one of Ken's past trainers and mentors, warrants special mention. She taught him the basis of the developmental approach we use. Her contribution forms part of the foundation of our way of approaching and understanding teenagers. We also thank the hundreds of families and teenagers who opened their lives to us over the years, who revealed what they were dealing with at home and were willing to give our suggestions a try. We have learned more from them than we can say about helping young people reach adulthood well prepared for the lives ahead of them.

Very importantly, we also thank the many people who answered questionnaires and read the manuscript in various stages of completion. We appreciate their generosity in answering so fully and making the many suggestions that they did. Their contributions have added a wonderful richness and clarity to what we have presented. They include: Mary and Roy Brash, Tim and Corinne Britten, Ros and Derek Broadmore, Nicole and Graeme Coppel, Mark and Sally Davis, Mireille de Meuron, Marc and Sharon des Landes, Helen Faulkner and Sam Lambraia, Peter and Jessica Garvin, Jim Hirsch, John Hofton, Vaughn Malcolm, Neil Mellor, Paul and Barbara Morreau, George and Jenny Packard, Nicky Riddiford and John Prebble, Vlad and Suzan Samson, Kathryn Schofield, Ingrid Stephens, and Martin and Sue Wells. Thanks also to Sara Parsons for typing many tape transcripts.

Finally, we thank all at Finch Publishing for their active, supportive, and professional contact through more than five years. In the final stages, Kathryn Lamberton edited the manuscript and contributed both precision and finesse to the final product. What you hold in your hands is fundamentally the result of their ongoing efforts to make truly informative books of excellent quality available to the community. We feel very fortunate to have been included in their authors' list. We continue to learn from and enjoy our contact with them and hope that our association continues for many years.

Further reading

For parents and other adults

Blum, R. and Rinehart. P. M., "Reducing the risk: Connections that make a difference in the lives of youth," *Youth Studies Australia*, December 1997.

Browne, Rollo and Fletcher, Richard (eds), *Boys in schools: Addressing the real issues— behavior, values, and relationships*, Finch Publishing, Sydney, 1995.

Carr-Gregg, Michael and Shale, Erin, *Adolescence: A guide for parents*, Finch Publishing, Sydney, 2002.

Doherty, William J, *Confident Parenting: How to set clear limits, be sensitive, and stay in charge*, Finch Publishing, Sydney, 2003.

Field, Evelyn M., *Bully busting: How to help children deal with teasing and bullying*, Finch Publishing, Sydney, 1999.

Garbarin, James Ph.D., and Bedard, Claire, *Parents under siege: Why you are the solution, not the problem, in your child's life*, Free Press, New York, 2001.

Green, Michael, *Fathers after divorce: Building a new life and becoming a successful separated parent*, Finch Publishing, Sydney, 1998.

James, Muriel and Jongeward, Dorothy, *Born to win: Transactional analysis with gestalt experiments*, Addison-Wesley, Reading, 1971.

Lamble, Jo and Morris, Sue, *Online and personal: The reality of Internet relationships*, Finch Publishing, Sydney, 2001.

Levin, Pam, *Becoming the way we are: A transactional analysis guide to personality development*, Levin, Berkeley, 1974.

Longaker, Christine, *Facing death and finding hope: A guide to the emotional and spiritual care of the dying*, Random House, London, 1997.

Mathew, Diana, *Money tree*, Money Tree Management Service Pty Ltd, Adelaide, 1996.

Mellor, Ken and Elizabeth, *ParentCraft: A practical guide to raising children well*, 2nd ed., Finch Publishing, Sydney, 2001.

Newman, Margaret, *Stepfamily realities: How to overcome difficulties and have a happy family*, Doubleday, Sydney, 1992.

Pallotta-Chiarolli, Maria, *Girls Talk: Young women speak their hearts and minds*, Finch Publishing, Sydney, 1998.

Ricker, Audrey Ph.D. and Crowder, Carolyn Ph.D., *Back talk: Steps to ending rude behavior*, Fireside, New York, 1998.

Sheindlin, Judge Judy, *Keep it simple, stupid: You're smarter than you look*, Harper Collins Publishers, New York, 2000.

York, Phyllis and David, and Wachtel, Ted, *Toughlove*, Bantam Books, New York, 1983.

York, Phyllis and David, and Wachtel, Ted, *Toughlove solutions: Runaways, sex, suicide, drugs, alcohol, abuse, disrupted families, community indifference*, Bantam Books, Random House, New York, 1985.

For teenagers

Bennett, Vicki, *Life smart: Choices for young people about friendship, family, and future*, Finch Publishing, Sydney, 2001.

Darvill, Wendy and Powell, Kelsey, *The puberty book: A guide for children and teenagers*, Hodder and Stoughton, London, 1995.

Matthews, Andrew, *Being a happy teenager*, Seashell Publishers, Trinity Beach, Australia, 2001.

Matthews, Andrew, *Making friends: A guide to getting along with people*, Media Masters, Singapore, 1990.

Wade, John, *Super study: A new age study guide*, Dellasta, Melbourne, 1990.

Webber, Ruth, *Split ends: Teenage stepchildren*, ACER, Melbourne, 1996.

Biame
NETWORK

Biame Network Inc. is an international, non-profit, educational organization. It is an Incorporated Association with members in many countries. Founded in 1984 by Ken and Elizabeth Mellor, its primary purpose is to take a spiritually based approach to helping people integrate personal Awakening with their day-to-day activities. The approach, called Urban Mysticism, is down-to-earth, practical, and easy to use. Anyone living everyday lives in the modern world can use it. The methods have origins in a variety of traditions, but owe no allegiance to any.

Currently "incorporated" in three countries and with programs in five, Biame Network has thousands of people actively associated with it. Its varied activities and programs enable people to use it as a resource for many different purposes. These include areas such as personal health and well-being, self-management, parenting, teacher education, relationship development, financial and business management, community development, personal growth and change, spiritual evolution and practice, energy healing, and advanced spiritual Awakening.

Anyone interested is encouraged to contact the Network. The organization is open to everyone, whatever their race, spiritual or religious orientations, age, or gender. Most activities are available to all. Both regular and one-time courses and workshop programs are offered in various parts of the world. A formal Training Program acts as a venue for systematic learning by people interested in exploring themselves more fully. Biame Network has an expanding range of teaching materials and other learning aids. All enquiries are welcome.

Biame Network
PO Box 271
Seymour, Victoria 3661, Australia
Tel: + 61 3 5799 1198, Freecall (in Australia) 1800 244 254
Fax: + 61 3 5799 1132
Email: biamenet@eck.net.au
Website: www.biamenetwork.net

Index